NATO'S
Defence of the N

BRASSEY'S ATLANTIC COMMENTARIES

Series Editor: **Eric Grove**

This new series will present a collection of introductory commentaries on important issues affecting the Atlantic Alliance and its future. The booklets are written and edited with the general reader as well as the specialist in mind and are intended to provide necessary background knowledge for the informed and continuing debate on Western defence. Among future titles planned are commentaries on WEU and NATO discussing the building of a European defence identity in the context of Atlantic solidarity; Spain's evolving role in NATO, the WEU and the EEC; burden-sharing and an assessment of the state of play in the fulfilment of the transatlantic bargains and the role of assistance within the Alliance in the development of the economic and technological well-being of the lesser developed member countries.

Brassey's Atlantic Commentaries No. 2
The Western European Union and NATO:
Building a European Defence Identity within the Context of Atlantic Solidarity
ALFRED CAHEN

Titles of related interest from Brassey's

GOLDSTEIN
Clash in the North: Polar Summitry & NATO's Northern Flank

GROVE and WINDASS
The Crucible of Peace: Common Security in Europe

HANNING
NATO: Our Guarantee of Peace

RIES
Cold Will: The Defence of Finland

RIES and SKORVE
Investigating Kola

WEST
Naval Forces and Western Security

BRASSEY'S ATLANTIC COMMENTARIES No. 1

NATO'S Defence of the North

Edited by

ERIC GROVE

BRASSEY'S (UK)

(A member of the Maxwell Pergamon Publishing Corporation)

LONDON · OXFORD · WASHINGTON · NEW YORK · BEIJING
FRANKFURT · SÃO PAULO · SYDNEY · TOKYO · TORONTO

UK (Editorial)	Brassey's (UK) Ltd., 24 Gray's Inn Road, London WC1X 8HR, England
(Orders)	Brassey's (UK) Ltd., Headington Hill Hall, Oxford OX3 0BW, England
USA (Editorial)	Brassey's (US) Inc., 8000 Westpark Drive, Fourth Floor, McLean, Virginia 22102, U.S.A.
(Orders)	Pergamon Press, Inc.,Maxwell House, Fairview Park, Elsmford, New York 10523, U.S.A.
PEOPLE'S REPUBLIC OF CHINA	Pergamon Press,Room 4037, Qianmen Hotel, Beijing, People's Republic of China
FEDERAL REPUBLIC OF GERMANY	Pergamon Press GmbH, Hammerweg 6, D-6242 Kronberg, Federal Republic of Germany
BRAZIL	Pergamon Editora Ltda, Rua Eça de Queiros, 346, CEP 04011, Paraiso, São Paulo, Brazil
AUSTRALIA	Brassey's (Australia) Ltd., P.O. Box 544, Potts Point, N.S.W. 2011, Australia.
JAPAN	Pergamon Press, 5th Floor, Matsuoka Central Building, 1-7-1 Nishishinjuku, Shinjuku-ku, Tokyo 160, Japan
CANADA	Pergamon Press Canada Ltd.,Suite No. 271, 253 College Street, Toronto, Ontario, Canada M5T 1R5

Copyright © 1989 Brassey's (UK) Ltd.

All Rights Reserved. No part of this publication may be reproduced, stored on a retrieval system or transmitted in any form or by any means: electronic, electrostatic, magnetic tape, mechanical, photocopying, recording or otherwise, without permission in writing from the publishers.

First edition 1989

Library of Congress Cataloging-in-Publication Data

NATO's defence of the North/edited by Eric Grove. – 1st ed.
p. cm. – (Brassey's Atlantic commentaries)
Includes index.
1. North Atlantic Treaty Organization-Scandinavia. 2. North Atlantic Treaty Organization-Europe, Northern.
3. Scandinavia-Defenses. 4. Europe, North-Defenses. I. Grove, Eric.
II. Series.
UA646.7.N37   1989   355'.031'0948-dc19   88-37011

British Library Cataloguing in Publication Data

NATO's defence of the North
1. Northern Europe. North Atlantic Treaty Organisation countries. Security –
(Brassey's Atlantic commentaries)
I. Grove, Eric
355'.031'091821
ISBN 0-08-037339-9

Printed in Great Britain by BPCC Wheatons Ltd., Exeter

Foreword

by the
Secretary General of the
Danish Atlantic Treaty Association and the
Secretary General of the Norwegian Atlantic Committee

THE NORDIC area is interesting for many reasons. If one looks at it in NATO terms, one thinks of the subordinate command known as Allied Forces Northern Europe, or AFNORTH, and the area it is responsible for defending — that is, Norway, Denmark and Schleswig-Holstein. In doing so, one inevitably begins to think of the Warsaw Treaty countries and their military forces close by on the Kola Peninsula, or across the Baltic Sea. It is, therefore, no surprise that Denmark and Norway were among NATO's founding member countries in 1949.

Yet, if one looks at the North as a whole, it is Nordic interdependence which emerges — five countries linked by geography and history yet quite distinct in their political relationships. Three of them (Denmark, Norway and Iceland) are members of the North Atlantic Alliance, although, of these three, one (Iceland) has no national forces whatever; two of them (Sweden and Finland) are neutral countries and, of these two, one (Finland) is tied by a treaty of friendship and co-operation to the Soviet Union.

The adjoining border between Norway, a NATO member, and the Soviet Union helps confirm this Nordic area as one of enormous geographic and strategic importance. A simple test with a map and a pair of compasses makes the point: draw an arc through the west coast of Norway with Moscow at the centre of the circle and consider the size of the area you have created between the axis which goes north to the Arctic and that which runs west to the south of Denmark. No wonder northern Europe is so significant from a security point of view (see Map 1).

Moreover, this is not a territory with broadly similar characteristics throughout. It encompasses widely differing features of topography and climate.

A few kilometres east of Norway's border in the North-East lies the largest naval base of the Soviet Union. Nuclear-armed Soviet submarines operate both there and in the Baltic. Soviet talk of making the north a nuclear-free zone has to be considered in this light.

Until the middle of the 17th century, Denmark was the dominant power in the Baltic. Indeed, as early as 1429 a Danish King, Erik VII, was able to introduce Sound Dues and to impose them on all foreign ships passing through the Öresund between Elsinore and Helsingborg. Then Sweden took over Baltic hegemony and later it was the turn of Germany to assume the same role. Since the end of World War II, the Soviet Union has been the major power in the Baltic. However, the Baltic approaches are controlled by NATO, and with them access to the Atlantic.

The authors who have contributed to this book touch upon these changes and contradictions and describe what they have experienced and witnessed while visiting the North. They tell of historical events, wars, weapons and lines of demarcation; and they write of the inhabitants who live and work in this highly-charged territory. They help to paint a human picture of NATO's northern flank which will be of interest both to the expert and to the reader who is merely curious to know how peace is preserved in this part of the world.

Peter Ilsöe
Secretary General of the
Danish Atlantic Treaty Association

Ellman Ellingsen
Secretary General of the
Norwegian Atlantic Committee

FOREWORD vii

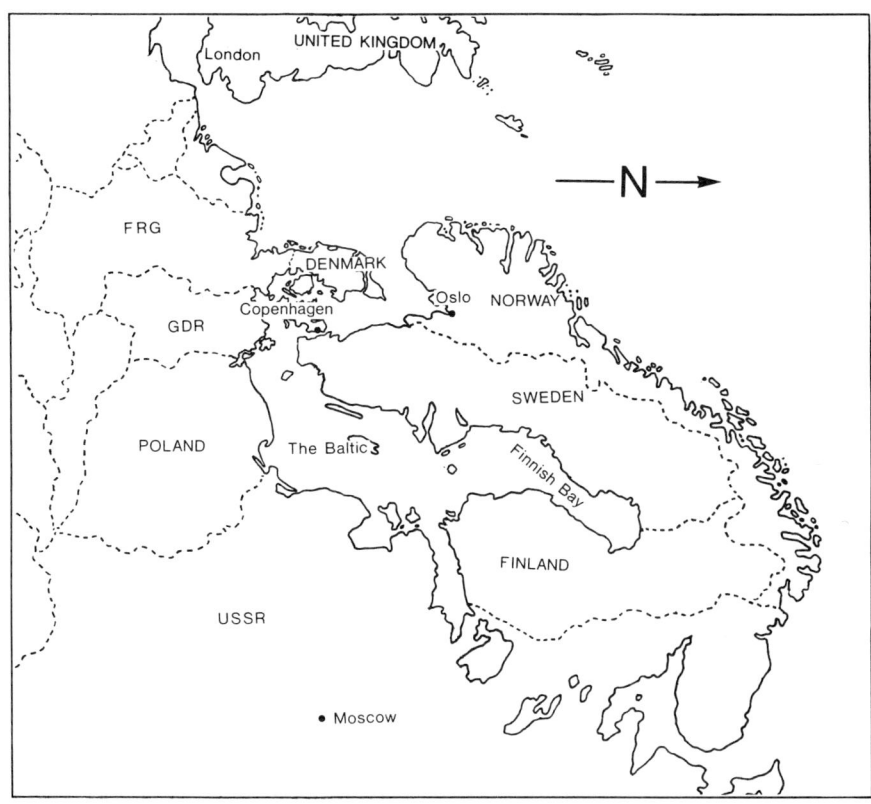

MAP 1. Northern Europe, the view from Moscow. The significance of the area to the defence of the homeland is obvious. Soviet defensive instincts have usually been translated operationally in rather offensive terms.

Acknowledgements

THE idea for this book was formulated by Nicholas Sherwen and Sjouke de Jong who commissioned the articles on behalf of the NATO Information Service while travelling with the authors in Denmark and Norway. The Editor would like to express his grateful thanks to them and to all those who have contributed to this work. Special thanks are due to the Danish Atlantic Treaty Association and the Norwegian Atlantic Committee: and to a number of individuals, particularly Jenny Shaw, Wilfried Hofmann, Robert Watt Boolsen and Irene Grove.

The opinions expressed are the responsibility of the Editor and of the individual contributors. They do not necessarily reflect the views of the Danish Atlantic Treaty Association, the Norwegian Atlantic Committee, or of NATO.

Contents

About the Editor and the Contributors   xi

Editor's Note   xiii

List of Plates   xiv

List of Maps   xvi

The Norwegian Sea — NATO's First Line of Defence   1
ERIC GROVE

Northern Lifelines   21
EDWARD FURSDON

Commandos in Action   43
EDWARD FURSDON

The Kola Fortress — I   47
HENRY VAN LOON

The Kola Fortress — II   61
EDWARD FURSDON

Baltic Strategy Past and Present   71
ROLF HALLERBACH

The Bornholm Story 83
ROLF HALLERBACH

Enough Deterrence to Deter? 89
ERICH HAUSER

Editor's Postscript 101

Index 103

About the Editor

Eric Grove works as a freelance defence analyst in London. For many years he was a civilian lecturer at the Royal Naval College, Dartmouth where he rose to be Deputy Head of Strategic Studies. Leaving Dartmouth at the beginning of 1985 to work with the Council for Arms Control, he later became a consultant to the Foundation for International Security associated with its work on the future of European Security. Amongst other activities, he is currently Associate Director of the Foundation under whose auspices he is engaged in a research project into Maritime Strategy and European Security. Eric Grove writes extensively on naval matters past and present. He is the author of the only major study of post-war British Naval Policy *Vanguard to Trident*, published in Anapolis and London in 1987. He has travelled widely in Norway and has developed a considerable interest in Nordic security problems.

The Contributors

Edward Fursdon was born in 1925. He has had a distinguished career, first in the British Army, from which he retired in the rank of Major General in 1980: and second, until 1986, as the Defence and Military Correspondent of the *Daily Telegraph*. During his army career he held a number of regimental, command and staff appointments in different parts of the world, including that of the Ministry of Defence Policy Staff Director responsible for European and NATO matters. As a defence correspondent he travelled no less widely, covering numerous aspects of national defence and NATO affairs. He also covered many operational and other situations abroad including the Iran/Iraq War, the Falklands aftermath and the situation in Central America. General Fursdon holds a number of academic distinctions and is the author of several books including *The European Defence Community — A History* (Macmillan 1980). He now combines his work as a defence consultant with writing internationally on defence.

THE CONTRIBUTORS

Rolf Hallerbach was born in Cologne in 1937. He retired from the German Army in 1984 with the rank of Colonel, after holding a wide range of planning and operations posts, serving *inter alia* on the staff of the German Military Representative to NATO's Military Committee. Since October 1984 he has been NATO correspondent in Brussels for the Defence Review *'Europäische Wehrkunde'*. Mr. Hallerbach writes extensively on military and security topics and has undertaken a number of important journalistic assignments.

Henry van Loon. Born in Paris, Henry van Loon is Defence Editor of the distinguished Dutch newspaper *De Telegraaf*. Arrested and deported in 1944, he escaped and returned to spend the last months of the Second World War on active service. He has been a correspondent for his newspaper in both London and Paris and travelled extensively. He now lives in Bilthoven in the Netherlands and is a regular contributor to the Washington-based magazine *Armed Forces Journal*.

Jules J. Vaessen. Born in 1932, Jules Vaessen joined the Royal Netherlands Navy in 1949 and was for several years a member of the submarine service in which he held three commands. After serving on the staff of the Navy Staff College, he joined the surface fleet in 1971 and went on to hold a number of senior appointments with the Netherlands Task Force, the Ministry of Defence and NATO's International Military Staff. Retired from the navy in 1983, Mr. Vaessen holds the rank of Captain in the RNNR. He has a degree in maritime strategy and is the author of a large number of publications on maritime strategy and submarines.

Erich Hauser was born in 1928 in Karlsruhe in the Federal Republic of Germany. An experienced journalist, writer and commentator on international and national political developments, he has been Brussels correspondent for the *Frankfurter Rundschau* since 1966. He is a specialist in European and NATO affairs.

Editor's Note

EVERY year, in early Spring, a small group of journalists from NATO nations visit governments and military headquarters in different countries of the Alliance to inform themselves about the security problems of the region. On one such recent occasion, after a trip to Denmark, Norway and the Norwegian–Soviet border, in addition to publishing reports in their own national press, some of the distinguished journalists contributed the material upon which this volume has been based. As far as was possible, the chapters have been presented as written but considerable editorial licence has been used with some pieces in order to create a coherent book.

First, with the help of the other authors, I look at the naval confrontation in the north and the growing importance of the area as NATO's first line of maritime defence. Then Edward Fursdon looks at the land defence of the Northern Flank, the vital requirement for reinforcement and the necessary interaction with the maritime and air situations. The General enlivens his account with colourful anecdotes of British forces on exercise in Arctic conditions. We then examine the threat in more detail, both in terms of the Soviet Navy and the Kola Fortress. The Dutch authors, Jules Vaessen and Henry van Loon, are our guides here. The latter then joins with Edward Fursdon to describe Norway's Northern frontier. Their vivid account well captures a unique situation that has to be seen to be fully believed. Then, in the able hands of Rolf Hallerbach, we move south and examine more closely the situation in the Baltic in its historical and strategic aspects. Erich Hauser fills in the political background. Interspersed with the chapters are small illustrative 'boxes' which are intended to cast light on specific aspects of the main subjects. Finally, I try to draw together the main themes that have emerged. It is hoped that the overall result will enlighten the reader as to how, despite various difficulties, a combination of deterrence and reassurance has worked well both to enhance the security of the Alliance's Scandinavian members and to maintain overall stability throughout the Nordic Region.

List of Plates

PLATE 1. The Keys to the Forward Maritime Strategy	6
PLATE 2. Close Escorts to Carriers	10
PLATE 3. The Core of the Anti-Submarine Striking Force — HMS *Illustrious*	14
PLATE 4. A *Typhoon* class Soviet SSBN	23
PLATE 5. US Marines during Exercise ANCHOR EXPRESS '86	25
PLATE 6. A Fast Attack Craft of the Norwegian Navy, armed with Norway's own Penguin Missile	26
PLATE 7. Norwegian Troops during Exercise ANCHOR EXPRESS '86	27
PLATE 8. Denmark's Home Guard in Action	30
PLATE 9. The AMF(L) deploys — Italian *Alpini*	32
PLATE 10. Searching in the Snow during Exercise ANCHOR EXPRESS '86	35

LIST OF PLATES

PLATE 11.	The USS *Hayler* leading STANAVFORLANT during Exercise TEAMWORK '88	36
PLATE 12.	Satellite pictures of SSBN Bases in Litsa Fjord	50
PLATE 13.	A Soviet *Hind* Armed Helicopter	52
PLATE 14.	The Soviet Strike Cruiser *Kirov*	58
PLATE 15.	A Golf II Conventionally Powered Submarine	59
PLATE 16.	Eric of Pomerania. King of Denmark, Norway and Sweden	72
PLATE 17.	Part of the Amphibious Threat in the Baltic: an AIST Class Landing Hovercraft	77
PLATE 18.	A Soviet *Terantul* Class Fast Attack Craft	78
PLATE 19.	Mining is Crucial to Blocking the Baltic Exits	79
PLATE 20.	One of Denmark's Vital Submarines	81
PLATE 21.	Soviet Troops in Devastated Bornholm	84
PLATE 22.	Another View of the Soviet Occupation of Bornholm	86
PLATE 23.	*Bredal*, a Fast Attack Craft of the Danish *Willemoes* Class	91
PLATE 24.	F–16 Fighter of the Danish Air Force	95

List of Maps

MAP 1. Moscow's view of NATO's Northern Flank   vii

MAP 2. The GIUK Gap   1

MAP 3. A Soviet view of Western barriers   5

MAP 4. AFNORTH   28

MAP 5. The importance of the Baltic Approaches to NATO   39

MAP 6. Airfields and Naval Bases on the Kola Peninsula   48

MAP 7. Soviet Ground Forces in the Leningrad Military District   51

MAP 8. Soviet Strategic SSBN basing and operating areas   55

MAP 9. The Memel — Mukran Ferry   74

MAP 10. Denmark and the Baltic Approaches   76

MAP 11. The Nordic Balance   90

The Norwegian Sea — NATO's First Line of Defence

ERIC GROVE

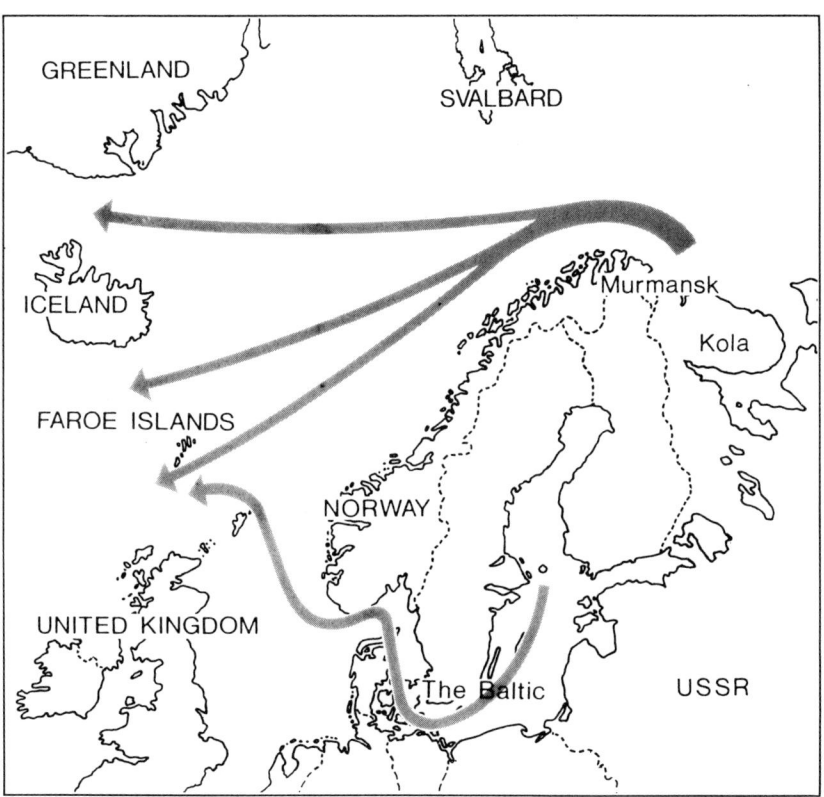

MAP 2. The GIUK Gap – the border area between the North and Central Atlantic.

DURING the 1980s the Norwegian Sea has become the focus of attention for naval strategists. This is because of the greater importance which both NATO and the Warsaw Pact have placed upon forward operations in northern waters. The Soviets have replaced many of their old Yankee class ballistic missile submarines (SSBNs), which had to make the dangerous passage through the Greenland–Iceland–UK (GIUK) gap to get within range of the USA. Now the giant submarines of the Delta and Typhoon classes can strike at the USA from 'bastions' in the Barents Sea, the Arctic Ocean and the Sea of Okhotsk in the Far East. Most intelligence analysts seem to agree that the main role of the rest of the Northern Fleet in war is the defence of the Barents and Arctic bastions using submarines, aircraft and surface ships. In classic Russian style, the Soviets have interpreted bastion defence in aggressive operational terms, pushing out a 'defensive perimeter' which not only looks as if it would include Norway well behind its front line but which would also put Soviet naval forces in a most favourable position to attack NATO's vital Atlantic shipping lifeline. The shape of Soviet naval strategy has been clearly displayed in exercises such as 'Summerex 85' (see box).

SUMMEREX 85

Rolf Hallerbach

SUMMEREX was an exercise involving the Soviet Northern Fleet. It took place in the Eastern Atlantic, including the North Sea and the Norwegian Sea, and lasted 18 days. Western observers put the number of vessels involved at 121 — 54 surface vessels, from aircraft carriers to frigates, 45 submarines and the remainder consisting of various auxiliary vessels. Powerful sea-air combat units from the Northern Fleet were used to provide air support. In the actual combat phase of the exercise, the operation centred on a defensive action against an eastward-advancing adversary. The defence consisted of anti-submarine barriers, already observed in previous exercises. When the attacking unit had come within 200 or so kilometres of the defending force, i.e. within range of the missiles, the defending force simulated a strike

> action co-ordinated by an air-based command post and carried out by the surface vessel and aircraft carrier combat group and bombers of the naval air-force.
>
> Experts felt that the exercise demonstrated more clearly than ever before that in the event of war the Soviet intention would be rapidly to take northern Norway, to gain superiority in the Norwegian Sea and, with anti-submarine barriers and powerful carrier combat groups, to destroy Western Europe's present naval warfare capacity. American carriers and amphibious combat groups would be engaged as early as possible along a line running from Iceland via the Faroes to the Shetlands and Bergen. This would secure the Soviet Fleet's long approach route from its bases into the Atlantic, which would pose a considerable threat to the Alliance's vital lines of communication with North America.
>
> Since 1985, the Soviet Navy has been considerably less active. The number of exercise sea days has come down from 456 in 1985 to 207 in 1986 and 114 in 1987. It is not clear what has been responsible for this development. The replacement and subsequent death of the ambitious Admiral Gorshkov by Admiral Chernavin, who emphasises close co-ordination of all arms, might have something to do with it. Alternatively, it might be part of Mr. Gorbachev's 'peace offensive' in the Nordic Area. It might just be because of shortage of resources and the need to save fuel. Whatever the reason, Soviet ship and submarine construction proceeds as before and the latent capability of the Soviet Fleet continues to improve.

Western navies have also revised their thinking, in part in response to this new Soviet doctrine. It must be emphasised, however, that the 'new' ideas of the 1980s are, as much as anything else, a re-articulation in a much more confident and coherent form of ideas that have been around ever since NATO's Atlantic Command was created in 1952. In MAIN BRACE, NATO's first major Atlantic exercise held that very year, the powerful Striking Fleet Atlantic, containing 4 American and 2 British aircraft carriers, appeared off northern Norway and flew off air strikes in support of the defenders. (It later landed reinforcements in Denmark and gave them support.) There was also much talk in naval planning circles at the time of using airpower from these ships to attack Soviet submarines 'at source' rather than wait for them to come out into the Atlantic. Both this idea, and the concept of sending Allied submarines to lie off Soviet ports in order to keep Soviet naval assets as far as possible away from the North Atlantic, went back to the earliest days of Anglo-American post war planning on how to cope with the Soviet naval threat.

By the 1970s, however, these operationally more offensive ideas had tended to be overshadowed by the concept of concentrating on blocking the GIUK gap. The main reason was perhaps the post-Vietnam decline in US Naval power and the doubts that the NATO Striking Fleet could be formed in sufficient strength to stand much of a chance against the growing capabilities of the Northern Fleet. Two things conspired to change the emphasis to a more forward posture once more. First was a feeling among NATO commanders that a dangerous 'Maginot Line' syndrome was being set up that was inappropriate at sea. A study was carried out to see whether NATO's basic defensive concepts, taken for granted on land, were applicable to the maritime situation. The result was the Concept of Maritime Operations or CONMAROPS adopted by the three major NATO commands (MNCs), Europe (SACEUR), Atlantic (SACLANT) and Channel (CINCHAN) for the 1980s and 90s. In the words of Rolf Hallerbach: the tri-MNC concept is essentially

> 'aimed at putting the crucial element of NATO strategy, namely forward defence, into effect at sea as well as on land. Forward defence at sea is not so much geographically as adversary-orientated. It involves sealing off the opponent's forces close to, or actually in, their bases (containment). Where this proves unsuccessful, enemy forces would be destroyed on their way to their theatre of operations in a series of repeated, graduated attacks (defence in depth). In this way, NATO would hope to be able to keep the initiative in order to prevent political leverage from being applied as a result of military inferiority.'

'Forward defence' in this concept was pushed beyond the GIUK. Jules J. Vaessen, an experienced submariner in the Dutch Navy before his retirement from active duty in 1983, describes how the Tri-MNC concept was interpreted in its early days as an extension of the barrier idea:

> 'The barrier concept is more than a mere blockade of choke points. It is a multi-layered system in which many different ASW systems all play their part. In times of crisis or conflict the general picture would look somewhat like this.
> - Surveillance of Kola reveals the arrivals and departures of ships, including submarines. Satellites in particular keep a continuous count of Soviet fleets in their home bases.

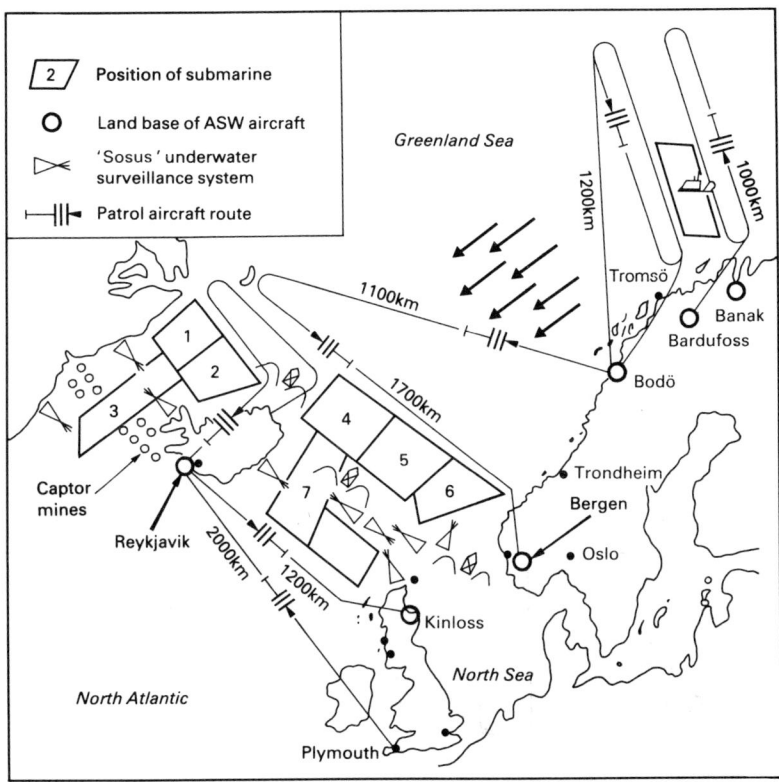

MAP 3. A Soviet view of Western anti-submarine barriers. From *Morskoi Sbornik*, November, 1976. (G. Till, *'Modern Sea Power,'* p. 60, Brassey's 1987.)

- Once at sea, submerged submarines are traced by listening devices on the seabottom. Known as SOSUS, these systems transmit their signals ashore where computers constantly monitor their findings.
- Nuclear submarines and maritime patrol aircraft form the next layer in the Norwegian/Barents Seas.'

This forward submarine barrier concept might well still form a crucial part of NATO's Norwegian Sea operations. However, there have been significant changes in the mid-eighties, both in a renewed emphasis on Striking Fleet operations and a change in the focus of the submarine battle. NATO's naval strategy has been pushed in these directions by the development of a new national 'Maritime Strategy' by the US Navy. This began in the early 1980s as Secretary Lehman's general rejuvenation of the service led to an attempt to produce a logical rationale for the '600 Ship Navy'. Again the drafters were not working from a blank sheet of paper but instead took existing plans and integrated them into a coherent whole. The new strategy was revealed to Congress in 1985 and was published in brochure form at the beginning of 1986.

PLATE 1. The keys to the forward maritime strategy. American carriers such as the *Theodore Roosevelt* seen here provide both the bait and the trap for Soviet air and submarine forces. Their likely location is the Norwegian fjords north of the Arctic Circle. Their aircraft are also vital components of the defence of Northern Norway. (*U.S. Navy*)

The essence of the Maritime Strategy was to set out how a power projection navy might be used to win the battle for sea control in, among other places, the North Atlantic. This meant an emphasis on the use of carrier aircraft and cruise missile equipped surface ships to hold at risk areas such as the Kola Peninsula. Even the possibility of amphibious landings was not ruled out. Illustrations such as the one here demonstrated the concept of operations in general terms. The US Navy was saying it was prepared in principle to take on the Soviets in their back yard, tie them down protecting that yard in peacetime and crisis, and if the worst came to the worst go into that back yard and win a limited conventional war.

The submarine offensive would be the key to the latter 'war termination leverage'. As Henry van Loon had it explained to him in 1986:-

> 'American attack submarines would not wait for Soviet fleets to disperse from their bases but would lie in wait and attack them at the harbour outlets, hunting down their Soviet adversaries in good time, even giving chase under the Arctic ice, "in a carefully planned and co-ordinated roll-back operation" says the Chief of Naval Operations, Admiral James Watkins, "with submarines engaging in single combat in the Arctic". The hunt would not of course be confined to Soviet attack submarines, but would be directed first and foremost against large Russian SSBNs equipped with heavy nuclear missiles. If the US Navy were to succeed in implementing this strategy, the Soviet Union would be stripped of a large proportion of its strategic missile arsenal during the first hours of a conflict — missiles which it would like to hold on to as a means of retaliation.
>
> One of the consequences of such a development might be for the West to reduce the priority currently accorded to escorting convoys and protecting sea lines of communications. Suggestions on these lines can already be heard. To quote Admiral Watkins again: "Convoy protection has seen its better days. It is in fact a very inefficient strategy, tying up many more ships than if we were to go forward and take the offensive against the Soviets".'

8 ERIC GROVE

See box opposite for explanation of diagram

> The U.S. Navy winning the forward maritime battle. This demonstrates in stylised form the way in which the U.S. Navy would hope to win the forward naval battle. This is the deterrent threat being manipulated in peacetime. Wartime realities would probably dictate many changes from this necessarily simplified ideal. From *The Maritime Strategy*, brochure issued with the January 1986 issue of *U.S. Naval Institute Proceedings*.

An American naval spokesman at AFNORTH in Kolsas confirmed this line of reasoning:

> 'We hope shortly to be so powerful at sea with our 600-ship navy that we shall really be able effectively to deny the Soviets access to the oceans. So long as Norway continues to enjoy its freedom, we can sail carrier groups far north along the Norwegian coast where they are protected to some extent by the natural coastline of the country as well as by the Norwegian Air Force, thus enabling us to pin down the Russians on Kola. What is more, if the American Strike Fleet is present in the Norwegian Sea, the Soviets simply cannot launch any attack against northern Norway. As things stand at the moment, we are a match for the Soviet fleet — in that respect I am not pessimistic.'

Perhaps that sums up the major change brought about by the Maritime Strategy, a new sense of self confidence that the Soviet naval threat can be contained. The previous paragraph also gives the lie to some critics of the new strategy who imply that precious assets like carrier battle groups (CVBGs) would be prematurely thrown away. In fact recent exercises have tried out the prudent placing of the CVBGs in large protected operating areas like Vestfjord where the terrain helps mask the ships from air attack and where the ships of the British component of the Striking Fleet, the 'Anti-Submarine Striking Force Atlantic' can keep Soviet submarines at bay. As it pointed out (in the accompanying box) Anti-Submarine Warfare (ASW) in northern waters is far from easy. The European Allies, particu-

PLATE 2. Close escort to the carriers is provided by impressive cruisers such as the *South Carolina* seen here. Nuclear powered, like their charges, such ships can cruise at high speed in the defended havens of the wide northern fjords without the need for replenishment.   (*U.S. Navy*)

larly the British, given their expertise in ASW, especially in the use of frigates equipped with highly effective long range towed array sonars, have a crucial role to play in the forward strategy.

ASW IN NORTHERN WATERS

Jules J. Vaessen

Norwegian waters are a submariner's paradise. The region is frequently swept by howling gales which make life miserable for surface ships, helicopters and aircraft. So much so that ASW operations become virtually impossible. Mountainous waves and shrieking winds, however, hardly affect submarines. Their domain remains calm and silent. Submarine operating areas in the North are often in or near the relatively warm waters of the Gulf Stream, rich with sea life, which sweep along the long ragged coastline of Norway. Beyond the North Cape they penetrate the icy waters of the Arctic. The Barents Sea is permanently partly covered by ice which expands and retracts with the seasons. Nuclear submarines can and do operate under it in a safe haven, conveniently close to the Kola, immune from all pursuers except their own kind.

Northern waters look pretty homogenous at first glance. However, the warm Gulf Stream waters do not mix with cold Arctic water or the fresh melting waters of the icecap. Unless stirred by long lasting storms, the water layers differ in temperature, salinity or density, deflecting sonar-transmissions and muffling noise — effective blankets under which submarines can hide. Such layers are also particularly prominent features of fjords and of the Baltic.

Another handicap faces submarine hunters in the fjords. The sheer rocky sides reverberate sonar-transmissions. If one imagines trying to chase a submarine in a kind of inverted cathedral in which noise and echo come from all directions, it goes some way to explaining why highly capable Norwegian and Swedish ASW forces search in vain for intruding Soviet submarines in their home waters.

The NATO 'ASW Striking Force', an ASW carrier of the 'Invincible' class and about a dozen British destroyers and frigates, plus about half as many more units provided by the other Allies, is almost as important as the American CVBGs themselves. Being effectively a European force the ASW Striking force is closer to the Theatre of operations in peacetime and can thus be deployed early in crisis both to demonstrate alliance resolve and to begin the 'precursor operations' for the CVBGs, finding and marking Soviet submarines — and any surface forces unwise to come too far forward. Thus is the early deployment of the big U.S. carriers facilitated by the activities of the European Allies. Moreover, Alliance solidarity is demonstrated in ways that do not raise immediate dangers of a super-power clash. In addition to the ASW Striking Force under Strikefleet command, the Commander in Chief Eastern Atlantic at Northwood in England has his own assets which he can deploy forward, if necessary. These include another British ASW carrier group as well as Dutch and German forces. French ships would also probably be made available.

The Commander of the Striking Fleet would like to have no less than four carriers with which to take on the Northern Fleet, but going into fjords helps make up for the absence of one and three carriers is a practical force goal. The Striking Fleet in general is a formidable asset, both in SACLANT's overall campaign for the Atlantic and in the defence of Norway itself. It doubles the number of interceptor aircraft available in Northern Norway, triples the number of all weather interceptors and triples the number of strike aircraft. It also gives options for nuclear escalation not available in peacetime. As Rolf Hallerbach has succinctly put it: 'Without the backing provided by the presence of the U.S. Strike Fleet, the navies of the northern European countries would be far too weak to offer effective, sustainable forward defense on the Northern Flank.'

The Norwegians naturally play down the Striking Fleet's nuclear implications, indeed the latter should not be over-emphasised at all, as the essence of the Maritime Strategy is how to conduct conventional operations to a successful conclusion. This very capacity could, however, itself raise Soviet fears of a usable offensive threat to the homeland. Some Norwegians, not least the present Government, have sensibly tried to reassure their powerful neighbour that no permanent American forward naval presence is intended. Thought has also been given to how a scheme of 'confidence building measures' could keep this growing naval confrontation under control. Examples might be a limit on routine NATO peacetime exercises to levels that could not credibly challenge the Soviet Northern Fleet and the Kola Fortress. This is normally the case anyway; exercise planners are doing well if they get two CVBGs to play with. Equally, however, the very regularity of NATO maritime exercises in the Norwegian Sea reassures friend and foe alike that the presence of powerful NATO naval forces when and as required is a routine feature of the Nordic Balance and not an unusually provocative event meriting some extraordinary Soviet response.

In fact many Norwegians have indeed been reassured by this new Allied interest in their waters and their defence in general. It is clear that they no longer lie behind NATO's naval front line. As the then Naval Commander North Norway, Rear Admiral Rein, (now Vice Admiral), told a conference convened by the Norwegian Atlantic Committee in April 1987:-

> 'A successful defence of NATO depends largely on the Northern Fleet being denied operations in the Norwegian Sea. To this end we need powerful NATO maritime forces in the area at the earliest possible time in a crisis to contain the Northern Fleet and thus prevent them from entering the Norwegian Sea. The NATO exercises comprising carrier battle groups in the Northern Areas in . . . recent years bring hope of a more tangible NATO commitment to early forward operations . . . we have welcomed Strikefleet's forward operations as an encouraging manifestation of NATO's potential to fragment the Soviet threat against North Norway, and to put into effect the recommendations in the concept of maritime operations . . . Thus the Strikefleet including the carriers have become elements that will impact directly in the Norwegian Sea to restore the balance in favour of NATO. From our point of view this is a vast improvement vice the earlier uncertainty to whether the carriers would be committed or just remain a strategic reserve in the Atlantic.'

Some critics express concern about an overly 'offensive' emphasis in all this. Serious questions have been raised. What if the Allied navies do as well as they seem to expect? Will it force the Soviets to use nuclear weapons against them? Attacks on Soviet SSBNs might especially lead to a nuclear response on the basis of 'use 'em or lose 'em'. Such fears are, however, overdrawn. Soviet statements make it clear that they regard the SSBNs of both sides as fair game in a naval war — hence their use of 'bastions' in the first place. The devastating consequences of American retaliation to the Soviet Union itself would also advise against premature use of SLBMs. In fact the balance of naval power in the North is sufficiently evenly balanced that the battle would probably be long and hard before anyone had a need to go nuclear to stave off overwhelming defeat. That is precisely the point. The new Western doctrines of early forward deployment demonstrate more strongly then ever before that the Soviets will have to make a serious fight of it in the North.

The main problem with the new 'forward operations' interpretation of CONMAROPS is that it might lead to a neglect of NATOs main priority,

14   ERIC GROVE

PLATE 3. HMS *Illustrious* (centre) is one of the British anti-submarine carriers that provide the core of the Anti-Submarine Striking Force, that operates ahead of the main Striking Fleet, defending it from hostile submarines. Two such ships are available for forward operations. One of their roles might be screening the deployment of the UK-Netherlands amphibious force in such ships as HMS *Intrepid* (top). Royal Fleet Auxiliaries like *Appleleaf* (bottom) provide replenishment at sea. *(NATO)*

the ships bringing to Europe the reinforcements and supplies that would be required both to start and sustain a period of conventional hostilities of whatever length required, wherever the attack had occurred. What if the Soviets decide not to play it by our perception of their book and the Northern Fleet, before hostilities begin, sends through the GIUK many of its submarines, perhaps those least suitable for the main fleet action in the North? NATO's naval commanders would then be faced with a number of uncomfortable dilemmas: forward operations or the direct defence of shipping? There might not be the assets for both. Captain Vaessen, both an ex-submariner and a designated convoy commodore, has little doubt that Admiral Watkins has been badly advised. In any future conflict, he persuasively argues, the convoy system would have to be resuscitated as the foundation of NATO's sea control strategy:-

'The name says it: the North Atlantic Treaty Organisation is a maritime Alliance. Its two pillars on the American continent and the Eurasian landmass are at the same time separated and connected by the Atlantic Ocean. NATO's existence is thus linked to the sea lines of communication between America and Europe.

Dependence upon the sea is nothing new: most of NATO's member nations are quite at home with it. The maritime nations of the old world have all waged wars to ensure free use of the seas upon which their prosperity and indeed their survival often hinges.

Naval warfare is but one of many perils that confront seafarers. Weather, shallows, pirates and collisions continue to play their part today as in the past in endangering ships, crews and cargo. Sea transport remains a hazardous business. Time and time again the gathering of merchant ships in convoys has proved an effective way of reducing risks. Ships in company provide mutual support and allow navies to give them adequate protection. Yet there is always considerable reluctance to resort to the convoy system. It is only accepted when there is no obvious alternative. Seamen, ship owners, port authorities and transport firms dislike convoys for a host of reasons, many of them quite valid. For one thing, seafarers tend to like their independence and do not want to be told where to go and what to do. Sailing in close proximity to other ships is something that sailors avoid if at all possible. Rational objections stem from the inevitable waste of time and resources which the system involves. Convoys assemble in remote places where ships have to go and wait for days, and sometimes even weeks, before the convoy is complete. At sea, speed is dictated by the slowest vessel, the route by strategic and military considerations. To add further to their misery, ships have to steer intricate zig-zag patterns instead of easy and sensible straight courses. On arrival, more delays are in store. Ports are swamped by large numbers of ships arriving at the same time and their facilities are grossly over-extended, until the rush is over, when they can lapse back into inactivity.

Insurance companies and wartime naval authorities are probably the main advocates of the convoy system. The former quote statistics showing that ships in convoy run less risk. The latter favour the system because they find it allows them to make optimum use of their overworked escort vessels. Naval units simply cannot be everywhere at the same time. It is doubly ironic in this context that peacetime naval planners often argue today that convoy is impossible because it requires too many escorts.

The convoy system, however, proved its worth in two world wars, dislikes and disadvantages notwithstanding, and was by far the most effective answer to submarine operations, air attacks and surface raiders. Despite continued anti-convoy feeling in NATO's navies, the lessons have not been entirely wasted. Contingency plans are in being to introduce convoys with as little fuss as possible in a time of crisis or war. The underlying philosophy is to let private firms and civil authorities get on with their every day jobs with minimum interference. Military and civilian organisations collaborate closely within NATO to devise the best structures and procedures.

The whole complicated machinery is rehearsed during NATO exercises when various parts of the organisations are called into existence to be trained and to test methods and procedures. On occasion, merchant ships are chartered so that convoys can actually be formed. That, of course, is the best possible way to test the system, but it is a fairly expensive one. When an exercise convoy is formed, the merchant ships are assembled and placed under the orders of a convoy commodore — usually a retired senior naval officer with considerable seagoing experience. He and his small staff will embark on board the ship best suited for the task, having adequate accommodation and communications facilities. When the navy, in the shape of the escort force, arrives on the scene, a convoy conference is called. Commanding officers and masters get acquainted and exchange information. They are told that the convoy commodore is reponsible for the convoy and the ships in it. The escort force commander for their safe and timely arrival. In practice this means that masters receive orders from the convoy commodore, leaving the escorts to deal with the enemy. Sensitive information like destination, route and radio frequencies is not disseminated at the convoy conference. It is handed out in sealed envelopes and only opened when at sea.

During its passage, the exercise convoy is subjected to all sorts of mock attacks and fake incidents. While the escort ships are engaged in their complicated naval manoeuvres, the convoy proceeds under radio silence with lights extinguished, altering formations and course as required. Participants are invariably pleased with the experience they have gained and the lessons learned. Merchant sailors in particular find it rewarding and useful training. The time-honoured convoy system, despite its sometimes unfavourable reputation, remains a viable and valuable tool in the Alliance's defence arsenal, and is still with us as a means of maintaining NATO's vital sea lines of communications.'

Not least of these 'sea lines of communications' are those which arrive in Norway and continue up the Norwegian coast. In such a potentially high threat situation there is no alternative to convoy for the merchant ships bringing in supplies to sustain the operations taking place on land and sea in Northern Norway. Just as these convoys support forward maritime operations so the latter take the pressure off the shipping in mid-Atlantic and the convoys in the South Western Approaches to the U.K. There is, therefore, no 'either/or' choice to be made between operating forward and running convoys, defending the Northern Flank or concentrating on protecting Atlantic shipping: the one requires the other. Both convoy escorts and carrier battle groups are vital to keep open the maritime reinforcement routes to the Northern Flank: and these, as Edward Fursdon explains in the next chapter, are its very lifelines.

THE OTHER SIDE OF THE GIUK

Iceland and NATO

Iceland and the United States concluded a defence agreement in 1951 under which the USA undertakes the defence of Iceland on behalf of NATO. As from the same time the Americans have had a defence force (Iceland Defence Force) at Keflavik outside Reykjavik. This force comprises a squadron of 18 F-15 Eagle interceptor fighters and a squadron of 2 E-3A Sentry AWACS aircraft for airborne early warning. The defence force furthermore includes a control and warning squadron which serves the control center for air defence functions and which provides early warning of air movements of interest within the North Atlantic area. For maritime surveillance and anti-submarine operations the force operates a squadron of 9 P-3C Orion maritime surveillance aircraft for search operations as well as 1 KC-135 tanker. A special unit responsible for defence of the airfield until arrival of designated reinforcements from the United States is organised within the force. The defence force counts a total of about 3,100 men. In addition about 1,100 Icelanders are employed by the force.

In order to oppose the growing Soviet threat in the Norwegian Sea in past years, Iceland had approved SACLANT's plans for improvements of maritime surveillance, radar coverage and air defence of Iceland. These improvements include modernisation of existing radar stations on the south coast of Iceland and building of 2 new stations on the north coast, shelter hangars for fighter aircraft and protected facilities for the command and control functions. The new measures also include that Dutch P-3C maritime surveillance aircraft with crews and maintenance personnel are stationed on Keflavik on a rotation basis and that also allied officers are integrated into the staff of the defence force.

The NATO base on Keflavik, including the defence force, plays a vital role, as far as air defence, maritime surveillance and early *warning of the whole Norwegian Sea area are concerned. In an emergency the base will be of decisive importance for maintaining communications across the Atlantic Ocean and for bringing forward reinforcements to Norway and Denmark.*

From p. 16 of 'The Military Balance in Northern Europe 1987-88' produced by the Norwegian Atlantic Committee, based on 'The Military Balance 1987-88' published by the International Institute for Strategic Studies, London.

Northern Lifelines

EDWARD FURSDON

CONSIDER the situation: just over four million people with some 90 per cent concentrated in the southern half of the country; a country over 2,000 kilometres long, much of it lying north of the Arctic Circle; 21,000 kilometres of coastline; a key strategic position; and probably the world's most powerful manifestation of military power situated between 10 and 100 kilometres of its north-eastern border.

Such is Norway's defence problem, which she cannot solve alone. But, by maintaining a basic core of modern and professional armed forces, and being prepared to mobilize the entire nation's efforts under a concept of 'total defence' in time of emergency or war, Norway is seen not only by a potential enemy but also by its own citizens to be ready and willing to defend herself as best she can.

Limitations of population and resources necessarily impose limits on the size and shape of the defence effort which can be maintained. Any attempt to match the defence resources domestically available against the potential military threat to Norway's survival as an independent country, taking into account all the above military disadvantages, inevitably leads to the conclusion that Norway could not survive a determined and well planned external attack for more than a short period.

There is only one way to redress this imbalance and that is to ensure that timely help arrives from outside Norway in the form of rapid external military reinforcements involving air, sea and land forces — in short a network of 'Northern Lifelines' extended to Norway by its NATO Allies. This fundamental concept continues to be the most significant rationale for Norway's continuing membership of, and strong support for, the NATO Alliance. Indeed such sharing and acceptance by allies both of the common risks to their freedom and the common burden of preparing advance defence against them, goes to the very heart of what NATO is all about.

In early 1986, the then Norwegian Defence Minister, Mr. Anders C. Sjaastad, was very frank about the situation. 'Norway alone is not capable of keeping pace with the Soviet build-up in the North. To make up the balance we have to "borrow" from our Allies. We have, therefore, made plans to enable us to receive Allied reinforcements quickly and efficiently,' he said.

General Fredrik Bull-Hansen, Norway's Chief of Defence until September 1987, recently stressed his view that the priority for Allied reinforcements was to concentrate on helping to dominate Norway's air space and the immediate adjacent high seas. He fully appreciated that the Norway-NATO relationship was based on common interest, and that if NATO reinforcements were to be successful in their primary tasks, Norway had to make a matching effort in defending the Norwegian land area from which they would have to operate.

What is the potential threat posed to Norway from the Soviet Union's extensive base on the Kola Peninsula? The Soviet Northern Fleet currently deploys 73 major surface combatants, 47 minor surface combatants, 64 mine countermeasures vessels, 15 amphibious warfare craft and 120 auxiliaries. There are 126 submarines, both nuclear and diesel powered, and 38 more submarines equipped with submarine launched ballistic missiles and assigned therefore to the operational control of the Strategic Rocket forces. At bases in the Kola are normally found about 330 operational aircraft for surveillance, strike, ground support and air defence, along with 100 helicopters and transport aircraft for both attack and troop delivery. The normal garrison is two motorized infantry divisions and a marine amphibious brigade. There is an extensive pattern of additional airfields, plus good rail and road communications into the Kola from the southern part of the Leningrad Military District which now make rapid reinforcement of the area a comparatively simple matter. It has been said, for instance, that within 24 hours an airborne division could be redeployed into the Kola and the number of aircraft stationed there doubled.

What then would be the likely initial objectives of such a powerful force at the outset of any hostilities? In addition to securing the Barents Sea immediately for the deployment of long range ballistic missile-carrying submarines (SSBNs) and the safe departure of some of these to their hidden lairs under the Northern polar ice cap, the first Soviet priority must be to win control of the Norwegian Sea. This would both defend the SSBNs' 'bastions' and be the first step in enhancing the ability of its Northern Fleet

NORTHERN LIFELINES 23

to pass through the Greenland-Iceland-Faroes gap out into the Atlantic to cut off Europe from North America. The outcome of this initial battle would be crucial for Norway itself, not only in ensuring the movement of Allied reinforcements into the country, but also in preventing the subsequent

PLATE 4. One of the occupants of the SSBN bastions: a huge *Typhoon* class submarine. (*Soviet Military Power 6th Edition,* March 1987)

encirclement and capture of the Norwegian homeland. These issues are all interdependent, the failure in any one could spell disaster for the others. The joint outcome could well thus determine the pattern of subsequent events further south on the central front.

NATO's naval forces must be capable of mounting and maintaining their presence in Norwegian waters in strength. Moreover, the continued use of key air bases and port facilities on the Norwegian mainland is vital for supporting any battle in the Norwegian Sea — just as the naval presence is vital in assuring continued use of those shore bases. It is essential to deny these facilities to the Soviet Union which would dearly like to use them itself to assist in projecting its own air cover forward from them. A viable defence of Norway is therefore crucial, particularly in the north — where such assets are vulnerable not only to strike and bomber aircraft from the adjacent Kola Peninsula, but also from Soviet amphibious forces and from the recently enhanced helicopter-borne assault forces stationed in that area.

The Soviet major naval Exercise SUMMEREX 1985 appeared to concentrate on developing and practising techniques and deployments for dealing with this Norwegian Sea battle problem — for example by establishing Soviet submarine barriers in the Greenland-Faroes Gap, and by co-ordinating with Soviet naval forces coming out of the Baltic to support the operation.

NATO's maritime exercises, OCEAN SAFARI, NORTHERN WEDDING and TEAMWORK, held regularly in succeeding years are designed to test and demonstrate NATO's ability to meet the new challenge posed by the extension of the Soviet 'naval front line' southwards from the North Cape further and further towards the Atlantic, even in peacetime. Exercises like this play a valuable part in strengthening deterrence.

The priority tasks of Norway's own armed forces are to protect Norwegian sovereignty over its territory; to offer the strongest possible resistance to any attack; to provide effective surveillance and warning and rapid reinforcement of forces stationed in vulnerable areas; and, in the event of a crisis, to create optimum conditions for receiving, protecting, supporting and co-operating with Allied reinforcements. In reality, Norwegian forces have to hold the ring long enough for external reinforcements to arrive in time to help them.

The bulk of Norway's standing land forces are stationed in the sparsely populated north, and are centred on Brigade North (which has its own

PLATE 5. US Marines come ashore in a landing vehicle during Exercise ANCHOR EXPRESS '86. (*NATO*)

armour and medium range artillery) in the Troms area. Two battalions are stationed in Finnmark. The northern coastal waters and the associated coastline is defended by a variety of naval forces and coastal artillery installations including fighter and maritime surveillance aircraft and helicopters.

In a crisis, the peacetime strength of Norwegian armed forces would rise from 37,000 (largely conscripts) to 325,000 including a Home Guard of 90,000. From its peacetime nucleus, for instance, the Army forms ten brigades in the 1st, 3rd and 5th Divisions in the south, two of which then immediately deploy to the north; and two brigades in the north which, together with the peacetime Brigade North, would come under the command of the 6th Division at Harstad.

The problem of moving internal reinforcements to the north rapidly enough is a difficult one because the country is long, mountainous and narrow. There is one major road and one rail link. These are strategically vulnerable and in any case would have to be supplemented both by an airlift and by sea transport through the archipelago adjoining the western shore-

PLATE 6. The Norwegian Navy includes powerful forces of fast attack craft like those seen here armed with Norway's own Penguin missile (left) specially designed for operations in local conditions. (*NATO*)

line. As it would doubtless be part of any Soviet contingency plan to sever these various vital links if it could, defending them is a priority task for the Norwegian forces. The recently implemented plan to pre-stock in Northern Norway the heavy equipment of one of the reinforcing mobilised brigades coming up from the south is therefore an important improvement.

But despite what Norway does for its own defence; despite its 'Total Defence Concept' and the mobilisation and involvement in defence of all aspects of society in times of crisis; and despite the subordination of all national civilian assets to the task of national survival, it is obvious that these valiant efforts alone would not be enough to hold off any determined all-out onslaught on the country launched by the Soviet Union for very long.

Norway's very membership of NATO and the presence of NATO's Northern European Command's Headquarters at Kolsas, some 15 kilometres west of the centre of Oslo, ensures that Norway would not stand alone in any threatened crisis. The very core of the North Atlantic Treaty, Article 5, spells out clearly that member countries agree to treat an armed

PLATE 7. Norwegian troops during Exercise ANCHOR EXPRESS '86. (*NATO*)

attack on any one of them as an attack on all, and commits them to taking the necessary steps to help each other in the event of any such armed attack. The NATO Commander-in-Chief Allied Forces Northern Europe, usually a British Army officer, would command all naval, army and air force units made available to NATO in Norway, Denmark and Schleswig-Holstein in the event of an emergency or war. During peacetime, it is his responsibility, through training and exercises, to ensure that his organisation functions

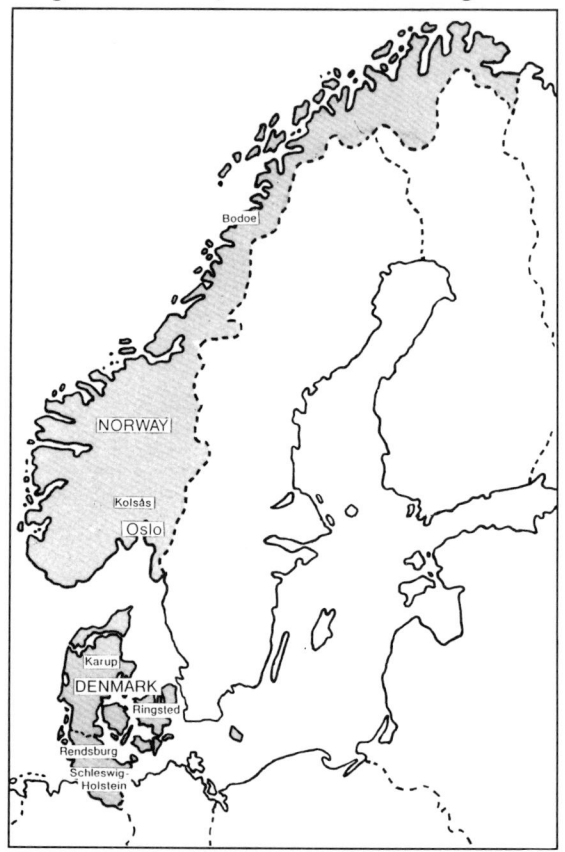

MAP 4. Norway, Denmark and Schleswig-Holstein constitute the AFNORTH (Allied Forces Northern Command) area. NATO instituted the current AFNORTH/BALTAP Organisation in 1961.

effectively and that the forces which national authorities will make available to him in an emergency are as proficient as possible in their tasks.

The Command's territory stretches from Kirkenes on the Barents Sea, adjoining the Soviet border, down to the banks of the River Elbe, and includes all the territories of Norway and Denmark and, in the Federal Republic of Germany, the Länder of Schleswig-Holstein and of Hamburg north of the Elbe. It is responsible for defending the exits from the Barents Sea to the Norwegian Sea, and thus to the Atlantic; the sea exits from the Baltic; and the vital direct lines of airspace connecting the centre of the Soviet Union with both North America and the United Kingdom.

In the southern part of his territory, the Commander-in-Chief's main problem is to defend Southern Norway and Denmark which together guard the Baltic exits. Current estimates suggest that up to six Warsaw Pact divisions could be launched against Southern Jutland, supplemented by airborne and amphibious forces.

A Soviet naval infantry brigade with 3,000 men and a Polish amphibious assault brigade of twice the size — both well equipped and highly mobile — are among the Warsaw Pact forces allocated to this specific area. The Soviet forces have recently acquired new hovercraft landing vessels and their operations could be supported by several hundred attack aircraft and helicopters.

Denmark's forces are not strong, with an active army strength of only 29,300 — but this can be mobilised to 104,000 in a crisis, plus a Home Guard of 78,000. Urgent and timely reinforcements would also be required.

It is important to note that Norway does not permit any foreign bases to be established on Norwegian territory unless there is a threat of war against the nation, NATO forces are not permitted in Finnmark at all. Denmark pursues a similar policy as far as foreign bases are concerned, though it is not officially defined as such. Neither of these two countries allows the stockpiling of any nuclear weapons or ammunition on its territory in peacetime.

The vital reliance of Allied Forces Northern Europe in general, and of Norway and Denmark in particular, on external Allied reinforcements has already been stressed. The forces which may be called upon to fulfil this role fall into two categories — first, the Allies' deterrent forces, and second, its specially tasked combat forces.

NATO's deterrent forces which could be deployed to Norway early in a

PLATE 8. Denmark's Home Guard in action.   (*Danish Defence*)

period of tension — subject to the Supreme Allied Commander Europe's (SACEUR's) and the Supreme Allied Commander Atlantic's (SACLANT's) priorities of the moment — are the Allied Command Europe Mobile Force Land (AMF(L)); the Allied Command Europe Mobile Force Air (AMF(A)); and SACLANT's Standing Naval Force Atlantic (STANAVFORLANT).

The AMF(L) is relatively small. It is a rapidly-deployable, multi-national, mobile, conventional land force with Headquarters at Heidelberg in the Federal German Republic. It only comes together as a force in the field when ordered to do so. If a NATO member such as Norway, Denmark, Greece, Italy or Turkey were to be threatened with attack in an exposed area of its territory, the AMF(L) would be dispatched to the priority area in question to make it quite clear to the potential aggressor that an attack on that nation — and on the AMF(L) — would constitute an attack on all

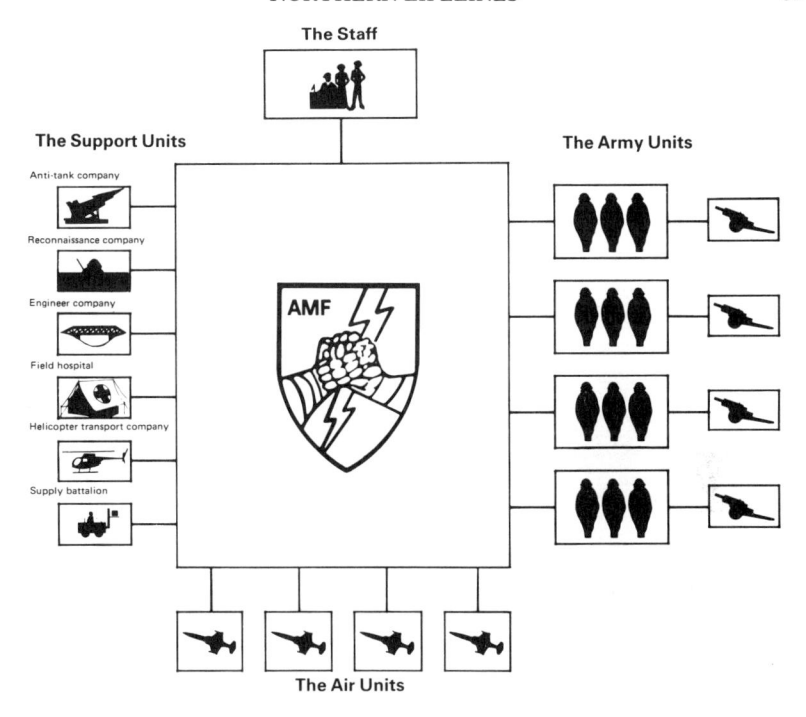

AMF – NATO's Crisis Force *(Courtesy of RW Bolsen)*

members of the Alliance. He should therefore think again about continuing his threatening behaviour.

Should this deterrent move fail, the AMF(L) is ready, equipped and trained to fight the aggressor force alongside the national forces under the command of the local national commander.

The AMF(L) consists of its Headquarters; an aviation detachment and an engineer company provided by the United States; a communications company from the Federal Republic of Germany; and an armoured reconnaissance squadron, a logistic support battalion, force artillery HQ, a battery of guns, air defence and locating elements, an engineer troop, a radio squadron, a force air support centre and an intelligence detachment, all from the United Kingdom. There is also a joint UK/FRG helicopter unit, and a composite military police unit. For the Northern region, a field hospital is

PLATE 9. The AMF(L) deploys. The troops are Italian *Alpini*.
(*Danish Defence*)

provided by the FRG, and the infantry units are contributed by Canada, Italy, Luxembourg and the United Kingdom. The mix of national units changes when the AMF(L) is deployed to NATO's Southern Region.

The AMF(A)'s air squadrons committed to Northern Europe are currently provided by Canada (CF-18 Hornets), the Netherlands (F-16s), the United Kingdom (Jaguars), and the United States (F-16s). It has no permanent headquarters or commander, and its squadrons remain with the national air forces in peacetime, coming together for exercises or operations only when so ordered. When this happens, all air units come under the operational command and control of the Allied Tactical Air Force or regional NATO Air Commander of the area to which they are deployed.

To present a credible and permanent demonstration of deterrence, the AMF(L) and the AMF(A) train hard and deploy on exercises every year. The fact that both are multi-national forces with differences in tactical concepts, operational procedures, equipment and language, and that they have to be ready to deploy to remote areas involving extremes of both climate and terrain, makes exceptional demands on all ranks. The importance of repeated exercising in such areas cannot be over-estimated.

It is also important that the populations of these rather exposed and vulnerable areas should see for themselves the evidence that NATO forces are prepared to come and practice their job on the spot. In the initial 'deterrent' phase of the AMF(L)'s annual exercises, particular efforts are made to establish good and friendly social, sporting and educational links with the local people.

The AMF(L)'s field exercises — known as the EXPRESS series — take place in one of its contingency option areas every year. Every second year this is in Northern Norway, Norwegian and other Allied forces join in for the exercise's final combat phases. ANCHOR EXPRESS, held in February and March 1986, involved 20,000 men and was the biggest ever held in Norway. It was based on the following imaginary scenario:

> 'During the late months of 1985 the relations between the North and South blocks deteriorated both politically and militarily. In January and February 1986 South stepped up the propaganda campaign against North, and early February South declared the Barents Sea as a military exclusive zone. Mid-February 1986 the

North Block noted increasingly out-of-area deployments by South Forces.

In this serious situation, the North Block requested AMF and external reinforcement forces to deploy to AMF contingency area North Norway.'

Tragically, ANCHOR EXPRESS had to be called off in the middle as a result of a very unfortunate and sad avalanche accident in which several Norwegian soldiers lost their lives, a reminder, if one were needed, of the appalling conditions which the soldiers have to face in this region.

ANCHOR EXPRESS

In March 1986, near Tromsö, General Fursdon crouched down in the field beside Private Chris Morgan from Cardiff in a raging blizzard in which the snow beat horizontally into their faces at nearly 80 kilometres an hour. Private Morgan belonged to the British 1st Battalion The Parachute Regiment, and it was his second 'season' with the AMF(L). "I don't really like the cold", he confided with a grin spreading over his snow-flecked face. But he was obviously thoroughly enjoying the tough role demanded of him as a member of AMF(L).

The same sentiment was echoed by soldiers of the Susa Alpini Regiment from Italy, the 1st Battalion the Royal Canadian Regiment from Ontario, and all the other nationalities, whatever their unit or task. Their unique AMF role was a tremendous challenge which they were determined to meet cheerfully and competently. The same feeling was equally apparent with the fighter pilots of the AMF(A) operating out of Bardufoss airfield where they were having to contend with the exceptionally difficult and fast-changing arctic weather conditions.

STANAVFORLANT is a small task group of about seven destroyers and frigates drawn from NATO members' navies. It comes under the command of the Supreme Allied Commander Atlantic. America, Britain, Canada and

PLATE 10. Searching in the snow during ANCHOR EXPRESS '86. Realistic exercises can sometimes exact a high price. *(NATO)*

the Netherlands are normally always represented in the force with Norway, Portugal and Belgium joining as and when they have vessels available. (Denmark used to be a regular contributor until it laid up its frigates at the beginning of 1988.) Nations rotate their vessels, thus spreading the experience of co-operating in a multi-national force, and of operating under joint command and control procedures. Joint techniques of communications, surveillance, tactics, operations, and logistical support are also exercised. The force would be rapidly deployed to a threatened area such as the Northern Flank waters in times of tension or crisis. In peacetime it participates in exercises and manoeuvres designed to enhance the task group's operational efficiency. It was deployed to the Baltic Approaches as a political 'signal' to the Soviet Union at the time of the Polish crisis in 1981–82.

The force is in permanent being in peacetime — either at sea or undertaking port visits within the NATO area on both sides of the Atlantic, or at times in the Mediterranean.

Under NATO's Reinforcement Plan, and depending upon other priorities facing SACEUR, important reinforcements could be deployed to Norway. Every Norwegian senior officer stresses that the reinforcements needed first and foremost are Allied aircraft. These are far more important initially than ground forces, hence the priority given to developing eight Norwegian airfields as Collocated Operating Bases (COBS) able to receive early American reinforcing aircraft. Arrangements are well advanced for laying on such items as ammunition, vehicles and fuel, and progress is being made in providing the necessary ground and technical equipment.

PLATE 11. In order to insert the Striking Force early into the Norwegian Fjords 'precursor operations' are necessary to find and, if necessary, deal with hostile submarines. In the recent 'TEAMWORK '88' exercise the multi-national Standing Naval Force Atlantic (STANAVFORLANT but known more usually as SNFL or 'Sniffle') carried out these vital operations. It was led by the newest destroyer in the U.S. Navy, the *Hayler*, seen here. (*U.S. Navy*)

An American Marine Expeditionary Force (MEF), containing up to 50,000 men with a very strong air component (160 fighter and ground-attack craft, 50 attack and 180 transport helicopters), 70 tanks, 100 guns and good air defence and anti-tank equipment, has Northern Norway as one of its priority commitments. In the NATO exercises held in Northern Norway every alternate year, the American force is normally represented by a Marine Expeditionary Brigade (MEB). In order to facilitate early crisis deployment of this MEB a major Norwegian scheme for the pre-stocking of equipment and material for it has been running for the past five years. Ammunition, trucks, heavy tractors, tanks and other ground force equipment is housed in temporary storage in Trondelag in central Norway, well back from the Soviet border in order to allay Soviet (and some Norwegian) concerns. Equipment continues to arrive and the intention is that permanent storage will be constructed in due course, paid for from NATO Infrastructure Funding. The project also includes extensive building and runway work at Orland and Vaernes airfields. The aim was to complete all the pre-stocking and other work in 1988.

The critical factor for the American MEF/MEB is the speed at which they can be transported across the Atlantic. 'Timely reinforcement' — in other words arriving in time to help Norwegians hard pressed to hold out until they arrive — is absolutely critical. Inevitably, part of the MEF must come by sea, but pre-stocking in Norway in peacetime allows as many men as an available airlift can carry to arrive early and become operational quickly.

The United Kingdom Mobile Force (UKMF) is specifically dedicated for the reinforcement of Allied Forces Baltic Approaches (BALTAP) — a subordinate commander under the Commander-in-Chief North, responsible for the defence of all Denmark and of that part of the Federal Republic of Germany north of the Elbe. The force forms part of SACEUR's mobile reserves.

The UKMF is a self-supporting expeditionary force of large brigade group size containing three elements. First, the 8,000 plus strong 1st Infantry Brigade combat element — stationed at Tidworth in England — consisting of four infantry battalions; a medium reconnaissance regiment with a guided weapons squadron; a squadron of Chieftain tanks, one medium artillery regiment, two light gun batteries and a locating battery; a Rapier battery and a Javelin troop for air defence; two engineer regiments; an Army Air Corps reconnaissance flight and a Lynx helicopter flight equipped with TOW anti-tank missiles; and normal brigade logistic units. Some 80 percent of the combat strength is Regular Army, and the remainder comes from the Territorial Army (TA).

The second element is the Logistic Support Group. This has a strength of 4,500 men (25 percent Regular, 75 per cent TA), and is primarily responsible for the 'in country' reception arrangements, the co-ordination of the 'Host Nation' support, the holding of war reserve stocks for a sustained period of combat, and for other non-unit level 'in depth' logistic support.

The third element is the Royal Air Force Support Helicopter Group from Odiham in England, which is an all-Regular force of five Chinook and ten Puma helicopters.

The UKMF has two principal options when reinforcing BALTAP. The Commander can deploy them to assist the Commanders of either Land Forces Sjaelland or of Land Forces Jutland: in the case of the latter, it could be deployed either with the 6th German Division or with the Danish Jutland Division, depending on the situation.

The UKMF's task is specifically one of blocking and strongly holding a specific area of ground around which other local forces can pivot and manoeuvre against attacking forces. Deploying by sea, the UKMF would be the first Allied operational reinforcement formation to arrive in its contingency areas of Denmark or Schleswig-Holstein and it exercises regularly in these areas.

BALTAP is like 'the cork in the bottle' blocking the Warsaw Pact's naval sea exits from the Baltic into the North Sea, and thus into the Atlantic to interfere with the reinforcement of Europe. It is also the 'link area' between Allied Forces Northern and Allied Forces Central Europe, the loss of which would effectively split these two vital NATO areas into separate entities. Operational cohesion would then be lost and the respective flanks of each area would become very vulnerable. In the Jutland Peninsula there are twenty key airfields, possession of which could effectively move the centre of Warsaw Pact operations some 500 kilometres westward. From there, they would bear directly on the United Kingdom. The role of the UKMF as a key part of the 'cork' bottling up the Warsaw Pact forces in the Baltic in time of war, is thus as strategically vital as it is obvious.

In discussion with the author, Major-General Gunnar Helset, a Norwegian who worked in the Allied Northern Europe Headquarters, stressed the essential importance of the UKMF formation in NATO plans. 'We would

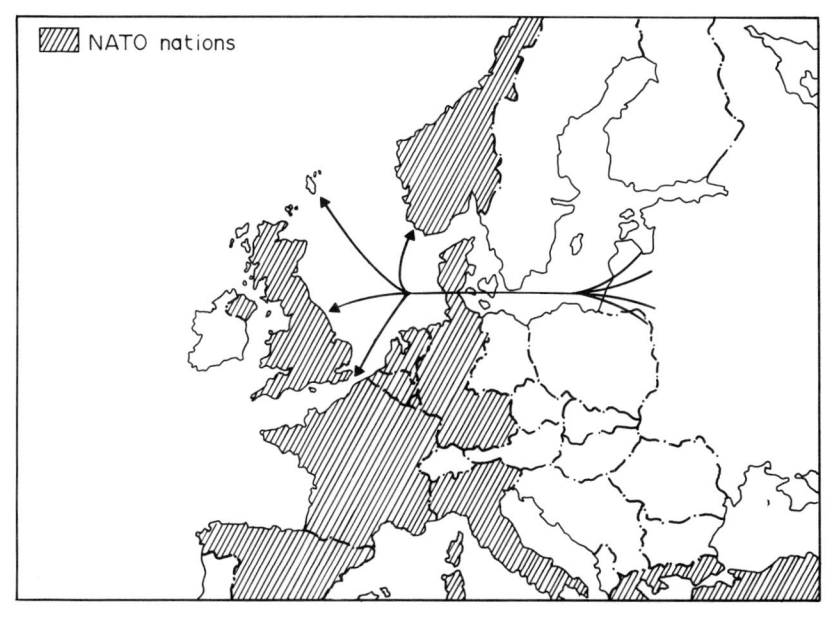

MAP 5. The importance of the Baltic Approaches to NATO.

very much like to see Britain upgrade this well-trained and very professional brigade into a division', he said, 'and also expand and update its equipment.'

Worryingly, due to developing problems, the commitment and deployment options of the UKMF to BALTAP are once again under scrutiny. A similar review for the Canadian Air/Sea Transportable (CAST) Brigade, whose Norwegian reinforcement role was exercised in 1986, especially concerning its rapid deployment, helped lead to the decision to re-allocate its Arctic trained units as reinforcements to NATO's Central Region. In order to replace this formation plans are in hand to create a brigade-sized 'NATO Composite Force' with units from several nations, including the German Federal Republic. Thus NATO solidarity will be re-affirmed, although the CAST Brigade's air assets of two CF-18 squadrons will be especially missed.

Perhaps the best known of the possible reinforcements to NATO's North is the Joint UK/Netherlands Amphibious Force of four marine battalions, together with all their necessary combat and logistic support. It is unique in that it is the reinforcement force stationed nearest to Norway in peacetime, and therefore usually expected to be the first to arrive — provided SACLANT is able to give it the North as its priority task. Its other advantage — for the present anyway, the future being as yet uncertain — is that it has its own amphibious shipping. Commenting on this, General Helset said 'It is very important that this highly professional force retains its own amphibious shipping lift capability in order to exploit its flexibility to take on whatever the operational priorities of the moment demand — be these tasks in Northern Norway, in Norway's Northern Islands or anywhere else in the Command.'

The force has to be amphibious 'in order to keep the Commander's options open', he said: 'This necessary operational flexibility would be largely lost were the force to have to use hired civilian vessels only capable of delivering them to established Norwegian ports.'

The Joint UK/Netherlands Amphibious Force — some 4,000 strong — is based on No. 3 Commando Brigade Royal Marines. The latter consists of a Brigade Headquarters with its associated Headquarters and Signal Squadron Nos 40, 42 and 45 Commandos; the Commando Logistic Regiment — which inclues a REME Workshop and a Medical Squadron: 29 Commando Regiment Royal Artillery with No. 32 Air Defence (Rapier) Battery: 59 Independent Commando Engineer Squadron Royal Engineers; 3 Commando Brigade Squadron: and 539 Assault Squadron Royal Marines with its Beachmaster landing craft specialised for Arctic operations and a Raiding Troop with both rigid and inflatable landing craft. The Brigade normally deploys with its Mountain and Arctic Warfare Cadre of highly trained specialists, 846 Naval Air Commando Squadron of Sea King helicopters, members of the Special Boat Section Royal Marines, and a Royal Navy detachment.

The Netherlands element of the Force came into being following an intergovernmental Memorandum of Understanding (MOU) signed between the two NATO partners in 1973. The Dutch marine forces involved are 'W' (or 'Whiskey') Company, which forms part of 45 Commando Group; and No. 1 Amphibious Combat Group (ACGT) which is about a battalion strong.

The whole formation trains in various locations throughout Norway every year from January to March in order to be fit for their Arctic role — as also does the British AMF(L) Battalion group. Most of this time is spent developing the vital skills required to live, survive and fight in appalling conditions such as blizzards and temperatures as low as minus 40 degrees centigrade. This is vital. It is only when a man has been thoroughly taught to fight and overcome the climate which is the main threat to his survival, and when he can move on skis and/or snow shoes with confidence, that he can turn his attention to developing his professional skills as a soldier and get to know the area in which he may have to operate.

At the end of every training season, the skills of all ranks are tested by major exercises. When commanding the force some two years ago, Brigadier (now Major-General) Martin Garrod stressed: 'It takes discipline — and especially self discipline — to conquer the elements before the man can start thinking properly about dealing with the enemy. And this training can only be done in the actual climate and terrain of Norway, where it can be seen to be credible both to the Norwegians and to NATO.' However, there is another side to the coin. Major-General Arne Rosnes, when commanding the Northern Norway's 6th Division described the north as a 'unique fortress built by nature', a potential 'friend on our side'.

The Norwegians are a tough, independent nation who know how to live in a hard climate and would fight to defend their land. Alone, however, Norway could not long withstand an over-powering and determined invasion of her territory. She will continue to need help from her NATO Allies to maintain credible deterrence in peacetime and should that fail, to fight for her survival as a nation.

The mutual interdependence of Norway's exposed but strategically vital geography and NATO's overall strategic defence of Western Europe and North America will therefore remain. Both for the Norwegian people and for their Alliance partners, maintaining these 'lifelines' is what belonging to NATO is all about.

Commandos in Action

EDWARD FURSDON

TWENTY-TWO year old Royal Marine George Smith, from Stanley, Co. Durham, was my host in his shelter dug deep down into the snow. Under the covering white camouflage net, our 'roof' was seven triangular white tent sheets clipped together and braced with skis. The walls and floor, of course, were of snow.

This experienced and lively Lance Corporal was doing his fifth stint of annual Arctic warfare training in Norway with 3 Commando Brigade. He was in charge of a detachment of Milan anti-tank guided missiles in No. 2 Section of 42 Commando's Anti-Tank Troop commanded by Lieutenant Chris Whiteley.

High up on a mountain ridge, with teams sited out in ambush positions, our exercise role was to cover a likely route for enemy vehicles expected around dawn. We were in an exposed area above the tree line, with plenty of deep snow. The Anti-Tank Section had been brought within reach of its position in BV 202 tracked over-snow vehicles. Within the ambush area such little movement as was allowed had to be either on skis or snowshoes.

Sharing the snow shelter with us were Section members Marine Andy Gatrick, aged 19, from Bolton in Lancashire, who boxes for both the Royal Navy and the Royal Marines; Marine 'Topsy' Turner, aged 20 from Beverley in Yorkshire; and Marine 'Fuzzy' Forrester, aged 19 from Preston in Lancashire. Being their first Arctic season, Gatrick and Turner had gone through the thorough novices' basic training course which teaches them, among many other things, the skills of cross-country skiing with a heavy rucksack on your back, on what the Royal Marines call 'pusser's planks'. If you have only done downhill skiing, this can be difficult, especially when trying to turn.

For a change, the night temperature in our hole was down to only -20 degrees Centigrade — 'quite warm', I was told — and my Royal Navy issue sleeping bag, rolled out on top of my thin foam mat, kept me very warm. Our rations were individual dehydrated 24-hour packs, well supplemented by the extra 'wets' (hot drinks) the climate demands. Lance Corporal Smith always kept a bag of clean snow in our shelter from which we filled up our mess tins as required. Heated up on privately purchased individual cookers, the snow first melted, and then came up to the boil. Dehydrated powder was then stirred into the mess tin and the resulting curry, chicken supreme, mutton or beef — according to which type of ration pack you were using — tasted especially delicious in these conditions.

In the very early hours of the morning, before dawn, the Anti-Tank Troop successfully sprang its ambush, the job done, and with the self imposed silence broken, we had to move off at once to another position to escape any counter- or follow-up attack. Working in the faint light, the weapons, the 'pulk' arctic sledges and the shelter sheets were very quickly packed up and we were off. A combination of high wind and more snow in the night had obliterated our previous 'safe' tracks and reference points, making it more difficult to extract ourselves from our exposed positions. One BV 202 vehicle chose this awkward moment to 'throw' (lose) a track.

By the time they got home at the end of March 1986, most of 3 Commando Brigade Royal Marines had stayed out on exercise in the snow an average of three or four nights a week for nearly three months. When you have experienced a little of it for yourself, you can readily appreciate how tough is the constant battle even to survive, let alone to fight, in the Arctic climate and terrain of North Norway in winter. You can appreciate how tremendously fit and professionally expert all ranks and all elements of the Brigade have to be in order to maintain the necessarily high standard of Arctic combat readiness its role demands.

Flying missions in support of 3 Commando Brigade was a Sea King helicopter of the Royal Navy's versatile No. 846 Naval Air Commando Squadron. I asked the bearded naval pilot — a veteran of the British military involvement in Beirut — about the problems of operating in the Arctic conditions of Northern Norway. 'The biggest one is the unpredictable weather', he said. 'It can change within minutes, and vary greatly even between adjacent valleys. It can produce extraordinary wind patterns and can close in very rapidly to create the exceptionally dangerous flying conditions of a total white out'. Lieutenant-Colonel Paul Stevenson, then commanding 42 Commando, later told me that because of the adverse weather, an average of only seven out of every twenty planned helicopter sorties might actually be flown.

For everyone operating in Arctic conditions, everything takes longer to do and the severe cold certainly tends to slow up the mental process. All of 3 Commando Brigade's different supporting Arms and Services have their own special difficulties with which to contend. 29 Commando Regiment Royal Artillery, for instance, has to cope with the fast-changing meteorology at the same time as worrying about the movement and deployment of its 105 mm light guns in the difficult and canalised terrain — especially the continuing requirement to get adequate ammunition replenishments out to their remote positions.

The actual siting of each gun down in the valleys has to be carefully worked out to ensure that shells will actually clear the adjacent mountain crests when *en route* to their targets. The effect of snow and ice conditions often muffles the lethal effect of different exploding shells and mortar rounds. At times, of course, guns may be fired deliberately in order to start an avalanche to block a particular enemy route.

Snow itself can be soft powder in one place, but yet have a thick crust in another only a few yards away. This gives 59 Independent Commando Squadron Royal Engineers problems when laying mines, especially mechanically. Some may end up buried and others not. Many anti-personnel mines are unsuitable in snow because they sink down into it under the pressure of a foot, rather than exploding. Grenades rigged to trap wires are often a better bet.

Water supply points freeze up in these Arctic temperatures and ice obstacles which have been cleared by blasting with explosives can re-form as they freeze again. Detonators can crack in the cold, and working with plastic explosives can be difficult. On the other hand, a combat engineer tractor, working near a landing beach, can keep a stretch of difficult nearby road ice-free by periodically soaking it with a load of sea water from its large front bucket.

For all units, starting up vehicle engines in the extreme cold is a persistent worry, despite the use of special aids, aerosols and pre-heaters. Battery life is reduced too, and some engine oils cannot function correctly in very low temperatures. Condensation can mist up key optical instruments and changing temperatures can cause condensation inside weapons. Once this freezes, the internal action locks solid and the weapon becomes unusable.

Nor does it take much for an unproteced rifle barrel to get snow packed up inside it.

Any handling of very cold metal is, of course, dangerous. The skin sticks to the metal and can tear off if pulled. One of the most frustrating aspects of winter warfare is that in extreme cold conditions the major task of maintenance and repair of vehicles, equipment and weapons cannot be undertaken on the spot, outside in the open, where the 'casualty' may have occurred. The skilled Royal Marine or Army tradesman from the Royal Marine Commando Logistic Regiment has to have warmth in order to work efficiently, especially for his hands. This means recovering the damaged items and taking them back to base workshops to work on them under cover.

Without doubt, the Arctic adds a special dimension to military operations and demands a different approach. The secret is first to learn how to survive by day and by night. It demands a combination of fitness and discipline, high morale, intelligence, teamwork, common sense and good equipment. Given confidence both in himself and in his equipment, the soldier can begin the thorough training which will enable him first to carry out his task in combat and then to fulfil his role in his specialist field.

Arctic warfare is a constant double challenge — for both friend and foe alike. The rules are harsher and mistakes the more perilous.

The Kola Fortress — I

HENRY VAN LOON

WHY are Dutch marines, British paratroopers and Italian Alpine troops earmarked for deployment in times of tension or war thousands of miles away from home in the Arctic region of Northern Norway rather than for the protection of Rotterdam, the Po Valley or the shores of Albion? To anyone who takes a look at the map of the world through Russian eyes, the answer is clear. Seen from Moscow, the Soviet fleet has only one really suitable, strategically situated ice-free haven providing unimpeded access to the rich hunting grounds of the Atlantic Ocean and the lifelines of the West. The naval base of Kola, with Murmansk and a number of smaller ports, is unique in this respect. Alternative approaches to the open sea are controlled by others: the Baltic Sea by the Danes, the Black Sea by the Turks and Vladivostok, on the Sea of Japan by the Straits of La Perouse, Tsugaru and Tsushima. The submarine base of Petropavlovsk-Kamchatski also has a number of disadvantages which make it infinitely less useable than Kola. It is extremely isolated, communications with the motherland are poor and all supplies have to be brought in by air or by sea.

Kola is, therefore, of vital strategic importance to Moscow for several reasons:

First, it is the home base for strategic submarines of the Typhoon and Delta classes which are deploying increasing numbers of ballistic missiles of the SS-N-20 and SS-N-23 types respectively. Both possess ranges of well over 8,000 kilometres, carry multiple independently targeted re-entry vehicles, and are much more accurate than their predecessors. The latter remain in service in significant numbers on the older Deltas and the remaining Yankees.

Secondly, from the Kola it is possible to launch an attack on Western sealines of communication. The Soviet Northern Fleet stationed there consists of about 200 surface combatants (including 13 cruisers), 126 attack submarines, over 300 naval combat aircraft and helicopters, and a naval infantry brigade.

And thirdly, with its 16 airfields and concentration of SAM missiles, Kola plays an important role in the strategic defence of the motherland. It lies exactly on the shortest air route between the USA and the industrial heart of the Soviet Union.

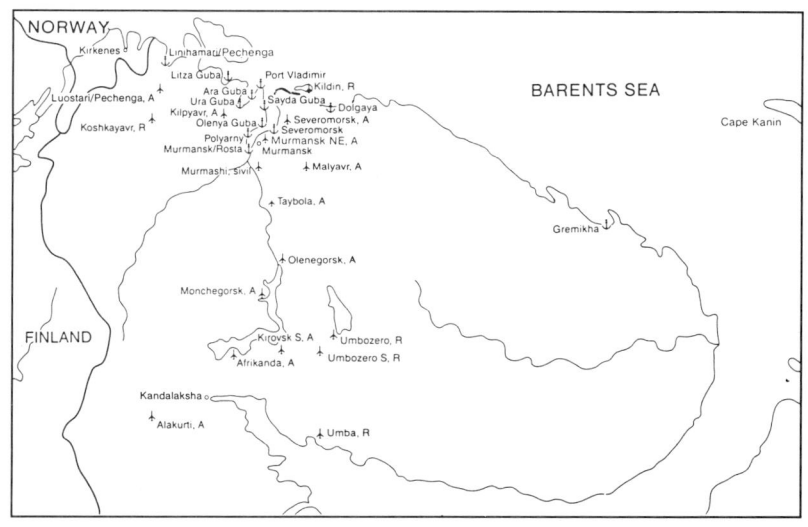

MAP 6. Airfields and Naval Bases ⊥ on the Kola Peninsula. Airfields: 11 active (A), 5 reserve (R) and 1 civilian. (Source: *The Military Balance in Northern Europe 1987-1988*, p. 25. Published by the *Norwegian Atlantic Committee*).

The protection of Kola and of its strategic submarines based there is therefore of paramount importance to the Soviet Union, but is possible only if it can control the Norwegian Sea and prevent NATO naval units from sailing into the vicinity. Over the past 20 years this control of the Norwegian Sea has been one of the prime objectives of the Northern Fleet. It now seems close to being achieved; during recent major naval exercises, Soviet ships extended their movements to the Greenland-Iceland-United Kingdom gap (the GIUK gap).

If the Russians wished to exercise effective control over the Norwegian

Sea, they would also need to have air supremacy and, in the absence of carrier-borne aircraft, they could only achieve this with fighters operating from airfields in Northern Norway. Only these airfields would give Soviet aircraft the necessary range to operate across the GIUK gap and over the central part of the Norwegian Sea, where the decisive battle with American — and NATO — forces would presumably take place. Without such air supremacy it would also be impossible for the Soviet Union to halt the advance of NATO by sea, northwards and on towards the homeland. All this means that the Soviet Armed Forces would have but one option in the event of hostilities, and that would be to occupy Northern Norway in the very early hours or days of conflict.

As a Norwegian Minister of Defence has bluntly stated: 'In the event of a conflict in Western Europe, in any conceivable scenario, the first attack will be directed against Northern Norway.' Should Norway fall into Soviet hands, the struggle for Western Europe could also have been decided. Hence the words of the American expert, Robert Weinland: 'World War III may not be won on the Northern Flank — but it could definitely be lost there!' So, in the snow and bitter cold of Tromsö, Harstad and Narvik, Dutch marines, British paratroopers and Italian 'Alpini' are, literally, engaged in defending Rotterdam, the Po Valley and the shores of Albion.

It is clear that, in the event of war, Soviet ground troops would need to occupy Northern Norway without delay — and this is where the first contradiction begins to emerge. Such rapid action requires preparation in peacetime — the stationing of A-category troops in the front line and the holding of regular military exercises. The Soviet Union is doing neither. More strikingly still, Moscow does its utmost to keep tension in Finnmark, along the frontier with Norway (all 200 kilometres of it) as low as possible. This is perhaps understandable when one recalls that the vital SSBN bases on Kola can easily be spied upon from north Norway and are vulnerable to unexpected attack. The observation made by the Norwegian Frontier Commissioner in Kirkenes, Brigadier-General Inge Torhaug, typifies this viewpoint: 'We are not allowed to take any photographs of Soviet territory: this is one of the stipulations of the Frontier Agreement that we have with the Soviet Union. But it goes without saying that we have ways of keeping well informed about what happens over there.' And from Minister Sjaastad: 'Our Intelligence Service does a fine job; we know exactly what is going on in the surrounding areas.'

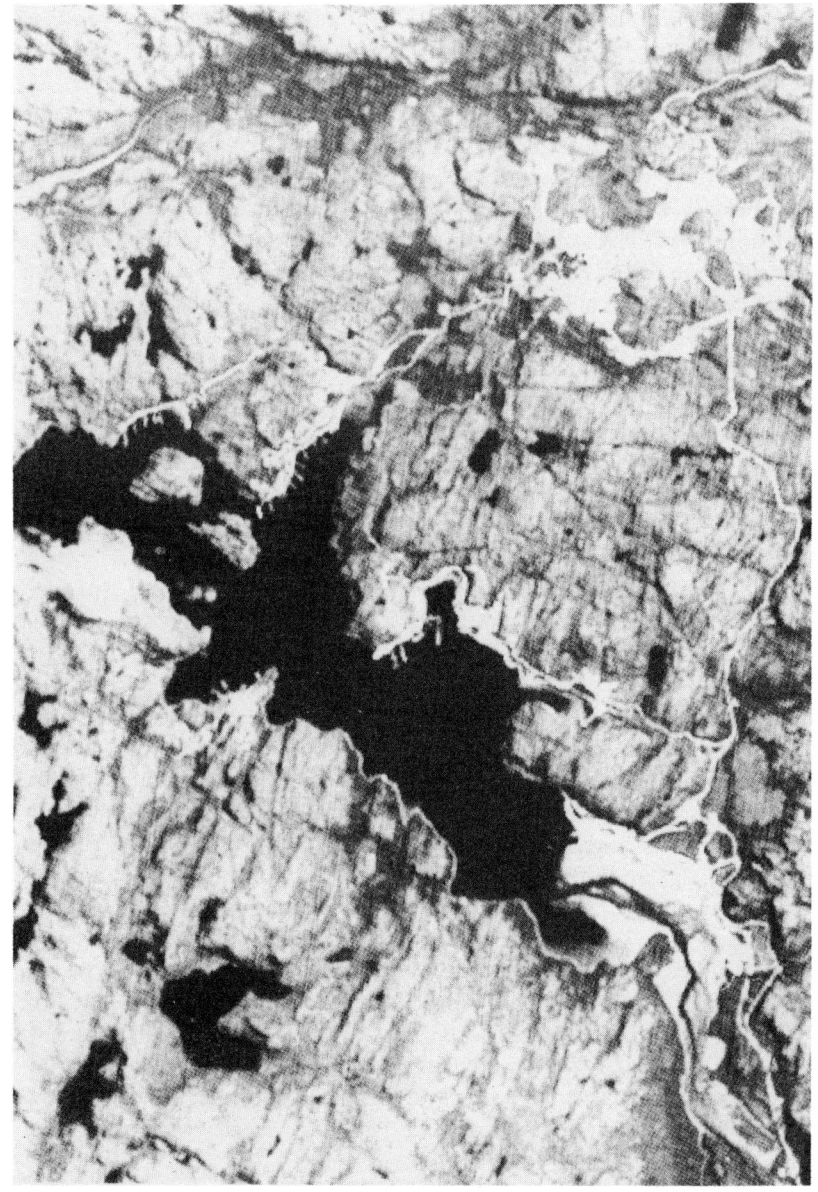

PLATE 12. Satellite pictures of Soviet SSBN bases in Litsa Fjord (*NASA picture from T. Ries and J. Skorve 'Investigating Kola', Brassey's 1987.*)

THE KOLA FORTRESS — I 51

The most important submarine bases on the Kola Peninsula are situated no more than 50 kilometres from the Norwegian frontier, but Norway has also consistently pursued a strictly low key policy — appropriate in the context of the Nordic Balance! The frontier zone with Russia is a 'no-go' area for Allied military exercises, no NATO bases have been established on Norwegian territory and no nuclear weapons have been sited in the country. Furthermore, the heavy equipment pre-positioned for an American marine

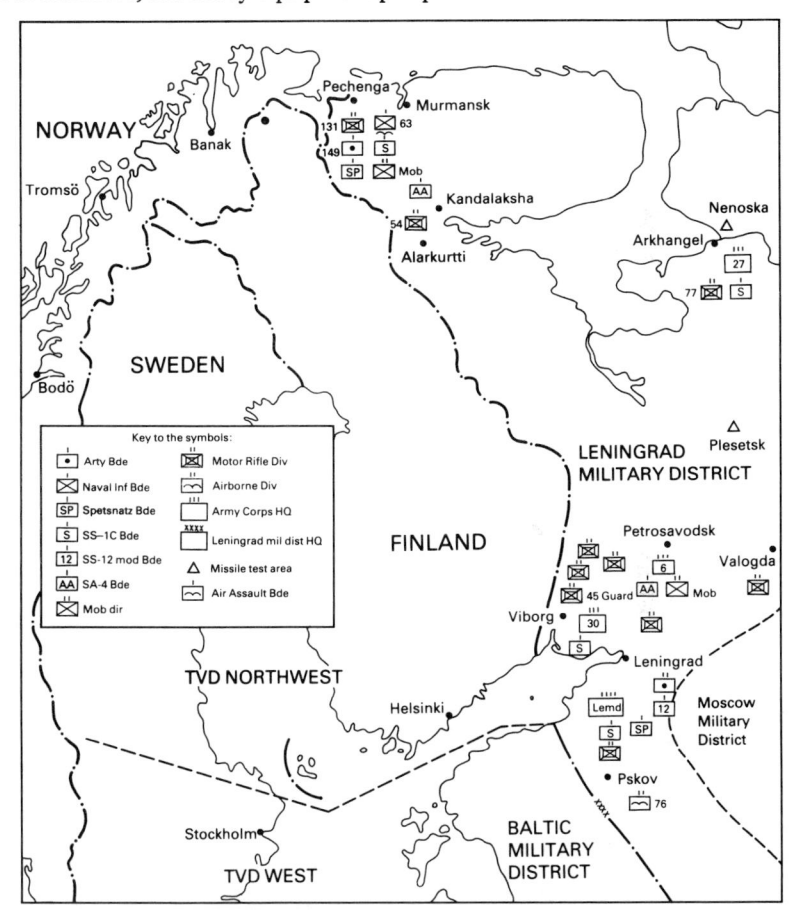

MAP 7. Soviet Ground Forces in the Leningrad Military District. (Source: *The Military Balance in Northern Europe 1986-1987, p. 24. Published by the Norwegian Atlantic Committee*).

brigade is located not in Northern Norway, as the military planners would like, but 800 kilometres further south. It is clearly in Moscow's interest for this situation to be maintained. There is consequently nothing to be gained by making threatening gestures towards Norway. The Soviets have resolved their dilemma, not by increasing the numbers of ground forces in Kola, but rather by improving their quality and making all the necessary preparations to ensure that Kola can be reinforced very rapidly. To this end, large amounts of equipment have been installed and a great many airstrips constructed.

Kola forms part of the Leningrad Military District (MD) which — in time of war — would be organised as the Arctic Detached Front, the ground component of the North Western TVD, one of the three continental theatres subordinate to the Western Strategic Theatre Headquarters in Kiev. The main task of the Arctic Front would be to attack Northern Norway and occupy it as quickly as possible.

The Soviets have available for this purpose the 6th Army with its headquarters in Petrosavodsk, and two army corps headquarters, the 27th in

PLATE 13. A Soviet Hind armed helicopter.   (*Danish Defence*)

Archangel and the 30th in Vyborg. The 6th Army has some nine motorised rifle divisions that might be mobilised in between 48 and 72 hours. At 24 hours notice is the 76th Guards Airborne Division with headquarters in Pskov and large amounts of air-portable heavy equipment. 250 transport aircraft and helicopters are available to the Leningrad MD, the latter including 100 attack and armed transport types like the Hind D. It is conceivable that Norway — which has only one main road running from south to north (the E6) — could be cut in two by an airborne *'coup de main'* aimed at Narvik, Harstad and Tromsö.

Based in the Kola area are the 131st Motor Rifle Division (MRD) at Pechenga and Murmansk and the 54th MRD in the area of Alakurtii, but to both are ascribed 'Category-B' readiness. The 63rd Naval Infantry Brigade from Pechenga (formerly Petsamo), on the other hand, is at a high degree of readiness. During the past two years this brigade has been strengthened (to 3,000 men) and modernised (armoured combat vehicles and tanks). There is more than enough shipping tonnage present on Kola to convey this brigade for an amphibious operation against Northern Norway. However, as the Norwegian Chief of Defence Staff points out: 'Although our greatest fear is that they will carry out an amphibious landing from Kola with a large armada of ships, the truth is that we have not observed them practising such operations. Their exercises are based rather on small-scale landings.' 'Nevertheless,' he goes on, 'let us not forget that they certainly have the potential for a mass landing operation'.

An attack on Norway could be carried out in two stages, beginning with an unexpected assault without any prior mobilisation, designed to eliminate Norwegian surveillance installations from the air with Spetsnaz units. These are special operations forces managed by the Main Intelligence Directorate (GRU) of the Soviet General Staff trained to conduct a variety of sensitive missions, including covert action abroad. In wartime, naval Spetsnaz teams would be transported to a target area by aircraft, submarine or surface ship and would be inserted immediately prior to hostilities. Once deployed, these teams of 6-8 men conduct reconnaissance and tactical operations against targets such as ship and submarine bases, airfields, communications facilities, ports and harbours and radar sites. Their training includes parachuting, scuba diving, demolition, sabotage, surveillance and target selection as well as languages such as Norwegian and English. Though a small force, Spetsnaz has the potential to achieve results disproportionate to its size against critical, yet often vulnerable targets. According to the official US publication 'Soviet Military Power', the success of these special forces in Afghanistan has led the Soviet Union to increase the number of units.

At the same time, the two Motor Rifle Divisions from Kola might march into Finnmark across the Norwegian border, where the Norwegians frankly admit: 'We would be unable to hold back an aggressor with our small frontier forces'. 'But', they add, 'our frontier troops are among the very best soldiers in the Norwegian Army, and they would be capable of inflicting heavy losses on the enemy by rearguard commando tactics.'

The seven divisions from the Leningrad Military District might advance from the Kandalaksha direction via the northern tip of Finland towards Skiboth, in order to occupy Northern Norway, perhaps even as far south as Bodo. This would, of course, be a flagrant violation of Finnish neutrality, so Finland would have to be occupied. Norwegian military opinion has no doubt that this would occur. The very existence of the Finno-Russian Mutual Assistance Agreement makes this almost certain. However, as Minister Sjaastad has said on the subject: 'There cannot be any Kremlin planners so foolish as to believe that the Finns would remain passive in the face of aggression — they are not like that!'

In this area the Finns have three peacetime brigades, one stationed in Sodankyla, one in Kajaani and one in Oulu, supported by an artillery battalion, an anti-aircraft battalion and two battalions of frontier guards. The war strategy of the Finnish Armed Forces consists partly of large scale guerrilla operations. As the adversary penetrates the densely forested and swampy terrain the objective is to harass and disrupt his lines of supply. Heavier mobile forces are then concentrated for decisive battle with the weakened enemy who is caught in a firepower killing zone. This general doctrine was used successfully in the winter war of 1939–40 and the Finnish Armed Forces now consider themselves relatively better equipped, especially with firepower than they were then. They are convinced that they can make Finland an even harder nut to crack in any future campaign. A 'Rapid Mobilisation Force' of 250,000 men, including air and naval units, is the first line of defence but no less than 700,000 men can be mobilised and equipped within a few days.

A Soviet attack on Northern Norway might emanate from a perception in Moscow that the threat to their strategic submarine fleet had increased as a result of a new American strategy. The US Navy Secretary, John Lehman, explained this to an audience of Scandinavian security experts in April 1985. The gist of his message was that, in the event of war, American attack submarines would not hesitate to attack Soviet SSBNs wherever they might be in the very first few hours. The latter might take refuge under the Arctic ice.

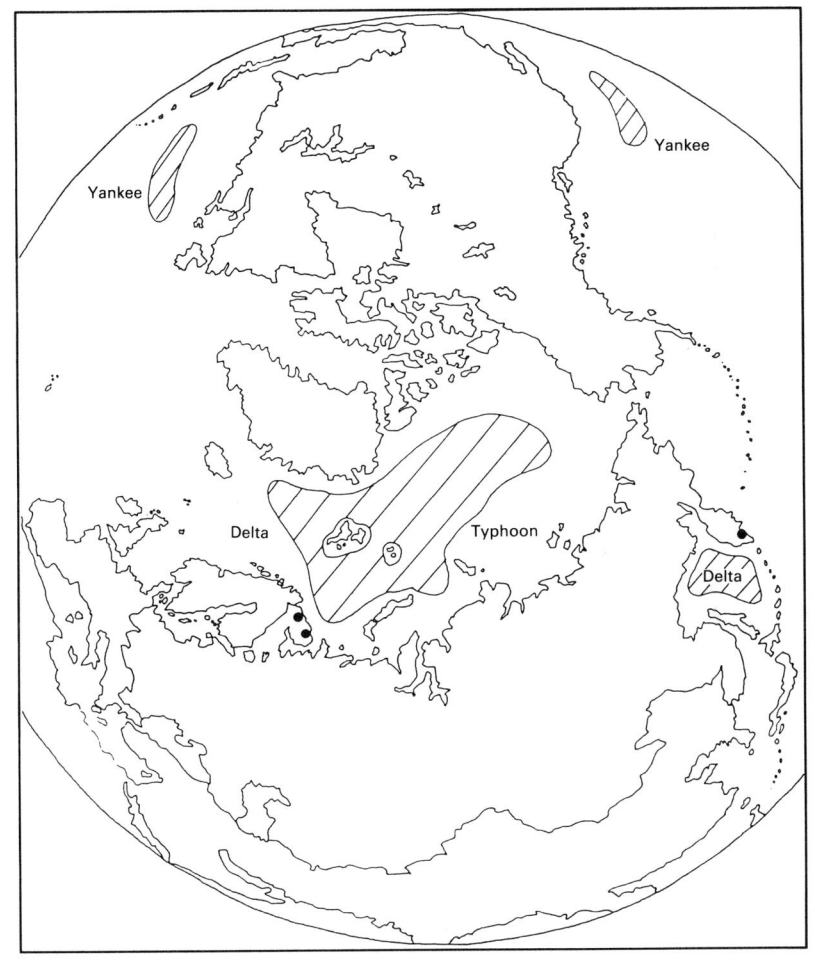

MAP 8. Soviet Strategic SSBN basing and operating areas. (Source: 'Investigating Kola' by T. Ries and J. Skorve, p. 27. Published by Brassey's 1987).

All this suggests that the Barents Sea and the Polar region will play an increasingly important role. The tracking of submarines is becoming more and more refined, thanks to British Royal Air Force Nimrod and American and Dutch Orion P-3 aircraft operating from the Icelandic base of Keflavik and from Scotland, Norwegian units flying out of their home airfields, and increasing use of SOSUS arrays (particularly in the GIUK gap) which register every underwater movement. The open seas are, therefore, becoming ever more dangerous for Soviet submarines, and they are consequently having to seek safety elsewhere. The Arctic waters are ideal for this purpose, since in those conditions detection systems function very imperfectly. Under the polar ice cap, additional factors come into play such as acoustic refraction due to the varying salt content of different layers of water. What is more, shifting pack-ice causes constant background noise and observation of movements under the ice is impossible. These constitute natural barriers under the ice which work to the advantage of submarines hiding there. It is, therefore, hardly surprising that the Soviet Union is showing increasing interest in operations under the Polar ice. At present there is no doubt whatever that the Soviet submarine fleet has by far the most experience in this field.

In fact, the latest Russian SSBN ballistic missile submarine, the Typhoon, is specially designed for this purpose. Four are already in service and there are a further three on the stocks. They are capable of remaining submerged under the pack-ice for months on end, awaiting orders to pierce thin layers of the ice crust with their fins, and, using their enormous weight to smash through it, fire their intercontinental missiles at targets anywhere in the NATO area. Every Typhoon has 20 SS-N-20 missiles, each of which carries six or more multiple independently targetable warheads to a range of over 8,000 kilometres. With a displacement of 25,000 tons they are the world's largest submarines — a third bigger than the American Ohio class. They have helped provide the Soviet Union with by far the largest ballistic missile submarine force in the world. At the beginning of 1987 the fleet consisted of 61 modern SSBNS carrying a total of 928 nuclear missiles. 21 of the SSBNs are equipped with 352 multiple warhead submarine launched ballistic missiles (SLBMs) with a range which would enable them to reach any desired target in the USA from the coastal waters of the Soviet Union. In view of these developments, it becomes increasingly clear why part of the Kola's unique strategic value is its proximity to the Arctic Ocean. They also explain why Admiral Watkins, the then American Chief Of Naval Operations, intimated in 1984 that American attack submarines had begun extensive training under the Arctic ice.

Northern Norway thus lives in the shadow of a superpower military confrontation that might conceivably make it the focus of a world war. Population statistics also create instabilities. There are about a million Russians living on Kola. Finnmark is inhabited by only 75,000 Norwegians — and, because of the demographic drift towards the cities in the south, even this number is on the decline. All the more surprising, therefore, that the Norwegian people do not appear to be really troubled by the dark shadow cast by their vast neighbour. But, after all, it has been there throughout living memory.

THE FOUR RED FLEETS

Jules J. Vaessen

WHEREAS NATO *is a maritime coalition — a fact of life not lost on the Soviet Union — the USSR is hampered by the unkind geography and climate of its own territory. With the longest coastline in the world, it only has access to the open sea in four isolated areas. These restricted and storm-swept waters frequently freeze over in winter-time. Each is the home region of a Soviet fleet*

–Barents Sea	–Northern Fleet
–Baltic Sea	–Baltic (Red Banner) Fleet
–Black Sea	–Black Sea Fleet
–Japanese Sea/Sea of Okhotsk	–Pacific Fleet

The really bad news for Soviet naval experts is that each of the exits into the world's oceans is narrow and is controlled by a potentially hostile nation. The concentration of forces, reinforcement of fleets and exchanges between fleets are all cumbersome and time-consuming operations which can be witnessed by the whole world. In times of crisis,

The **Black Sea Fleet** has the second biggest concentration of Soviet naval shipbuilding yards. The Black Sea Fleet protects the USSR's southern flank and provides most of the surface ships for the Mediterranean squadron. Free passage of its submarines through the Dardanelles is prohibited by the Montreux Convention. Some of the Black Sea Fleet is deployed in the Caspian: 4 large surface units, 5 small, 25 mine countermeasures units, 3 amphibious vessels and 7 auxiliaries.

The **Pacific Fleet** covers the eastern shores of the Soviet empire. It is closest to the sealines across the Pacific and keeps a watchful eye on the Japanese and Chinese naval forces. About 3 submarines, 6-8 surface combatants, an amphibious ship and up to 12 auxiliaries are normally forward deployed at Cam Ranh Bay, Vietnam. The Fleet also provides the units for the squadron in the Indian Ocean: on average this consists of a submarine, 2-4 surface combatants, an amphibious ship and about 7 auxiliaries. With the Northern Fleet it shares the main responsibility for the SSBN force, the nation's nuclear strategic second strike capability. Like the Baltic Fleet it is hampered by severe ice conditions in the long winter season.

The Kola Fortress — II

EDWARD FURSDON

(Adapted from an article first printed in the Army Quarterly and Defence Journal. By courtesy of the publishers.)

IF I had been allowed to cross the Norwegian-Soviet border on a fast motorbike after an early breakfast, I could have ridden to the big Soviet Naval Base at Pechanga, circulated around the eight major strategic submarine bases in the west of the Kola Peninsula, taken in a few of the new major airfields, and have been either back across the border, or have ridden on down to Murmansk, in time for a late lunch.

It is no surprise, therefore, that the proximity of these vital Soviet bases to the border — the nearest is only six miles (10 kilometres) away and nearly all are within 60 miles (100 kilometres) of it — has a profound effect on both Soviet and Norwegian defence thoughts and plans for the area.

But, looking into the Soviet Union, it struck me strongly that the blanket of snow lying over the low hills and frozen lakes, and outlining the branches of the trees in the valley's sparse spinneys, lay just as snugly on the Soviet as on the Norwegian side — its continuous unbroken surface knowing nothing of frontiers or ideologies.

Within NATO, only Norway and Turkey, situated at the northern and southern extremities of the Alliance's flanks, have a common border with the Soviet Union. Norway's run south from the Barents Sea, east of Kirkenes, for 120 miles (196 kilometres) before linking up with the Finnish-Soviet Border. Since the 12th century there has been recorded free interchange between Scandinavia and Russia in the Finnmark, Kola and Archangel areas. The last time a Norwegian tax collector went to Archangel was in 1813. It was only in 1826 that, for the very first time, Norway and Russia agreed on an official border between the two countries.

The prime object of both the Norwegian and Soviet governments in the sensitive area of Norwegian Finnmark and the Russian Kola Peninsula is to maintain the status quo, not rock the boat, and keep the common border area undramatic and very low key. Press and television media members arriving and requesting provocative pictures of Norwegian soldiers jumping out of helicopters and running towards the border, or pointing their weapons towards it, are sent on their way disappointed.

There is only one legal border crossing point — the tiny post at Storskog, east of Kirkenes. The Border Commissioner, Norwegian Air Force Brigadier Inge. A. Torhaug told me that his relations with his Soviet opposite number, a Lieutenant-Colonel in the KGB Border Guards, were 'relaxed, good and correct under the terms of the detailed Border Agreement signed between the two Governments in 1949'.

The Agreement's provisions covered a wide spectrum of activity. The first part deals with the actual border markers, the no-man's land in between them, and the question of the maintenance of both. The second part covers the use of boats and matters of fishing on the border lakes and rivers. For instance no foreigner can either fish or use a boat in the border area. Part three lays down the agreed rules for hunting, shooting, agriculture and mining.

Perhaps the most interesting part comes next. It deals with actual border crossings and behaviour, and the prevention of episodes or incidents at the crossing point or in the border area generally. It specifies that there can be no crossing, no contacts or any communication whatsoever across the border without the express prior approval of both Commissioners. No photography of any part of either side's territory is permitted, and no rude, insulting or derogatory sign or gesture may be made by anyone directed towards the other side.

Infringement of these conditions is swiftly dealt with by the police, and offenders are punished, normally by fines, photographers have their films confiscated. I saw for myself just how alert the border sentries are, and the speed at which they can react against any transgressor.

The actual 120 miles length of border is marked by 415 pairs of numbered 'poles' distanced from each other by line of sight. They are $1\frac{1}{2}$ metres high, and are set out opposite each other four metres apart — each one being exactly two metres from the accepted border line on the ground. The Norwegian 'poles' are yellow, with their pointed tops painted black. The Soviet ones have alternate red and green horizontal bands — five red and four green — with the top painted red. Set back from the lines of 'poles' are border observation towers, but not all of these are continuously manned. The Russians have 100 and the Norwegians have 12.

In fact there are relatively few official border crossings in the year, and these fall into four categories. First, there are the official delegations coming across on formal visits. Second are cross-border trade goods and materials. Third, interchange visits and supporting team exchanges arranged for Norwegian and Soviet youth groups either from Kirkenes or from the Nikel and Murmansk local areas. Fourth are a limited number of tourists from Europe visiting the Soviet Union — normally Murmansk — and I met a Norwegian doctor and his wife from Oslo who were doing this. Crossing at Storskog, the tourist parties are met by an Intourist bus on the Soviet side which drives them south to Nikel. They then travel on very slowly by night by train to arrive in Murmansk in the early morning.

The Soviet side of the border with Norway is controlled by some 850 KGB Border Guards. A controlled zone extends back up to three miles (5 kilometres) from the line of border 'poles' or the border river. Its rear boundary is marked by a double barbed wire fence, and entry into the zone is only through gates normally kept locked. Sensors are deployed to detect any intruder movement: the zone is constantly patrolled, but there are no mines.

Responsibility for the Norwegian side of the border — and also for the defence of South Varanger — is that of a 550-strong Norwegian Army Infantry Battalion stationed just west of Kirkenes. The commanding officer, Lieutenant-Colonel Ola Petter Løvlien, told me that he mans seven border stations with about 150 men at any one time.

The Battalion's Border Company controls the border area by manning observation towers, and by day and night patrolling on foot, bicycle, boat, skis, snow scooter or, at times by helicopter. The men are trained and well-equipped to stay out for days on end.

All the soldiers in the Battalion are hand-picked national service volunteers of above average physical fitness and intelligence. They start with three months basic training in Southern Norway. This is followed by a further three to six months training in a rifle company within the Battalion during which the men learn their infantry skills and increase their fitness. Only after this can they be selected for and appointed to the Border Company for their last three to six months of conscript service. By contrast, many of the Battalion's officers at the time of my visit were serving on second or third tours in South Varanger. They know the area intimately, are highly trained in the specialised type of fighting that the unusual terrain demands, and are used to a 'Midnight Sun' lasting from mid-May to mid-July every year.

I visited two soldiers manning a border observation post at Skafferhullet by the Pasvik River, which is where a loop of Soviet territory bulges out into that of Norway. This irregularity in the border line originates from the presence of a Russian Orthodox chapel built in the village of Boris Gleb in the 1550s, which would otherwise have been absorbed into Norway at the time the border was first agreed. The post looks across to the Soviet power station in Boris Gleb, where 20 civilians and 15 Soviet Border Guards live and work. The site was visited by Mr. Khruschev himself in 1961. There are, in fact, four power stations along the river line, two Soviet and two Norwegian, but all have been built by a Norwegian contractor.

The Skafferhullet post is one of several points — including two permanently manned observation towers — in a sector controlled by the Elvenes Border Station. The station commander, Lieutenant Lekven, said that he had 17 miles (27 kilometres) of border to look after 'as the crow flies' but, due to the nature of the terrain, it was 31 miles (50 kilometres) long in practical patrolling terms. There were 87 pairs of border marking 'poles' in his area, and each of his observation towers was manned by a team of four soldiers — one of whom was a Corporal — which he changed over every fortnight.

Commenting on his other operational role of defending South Varanger, Colonel Løvlien said that although he could be quite quickly reinforced, he had to plan on the Battalion initially having to operate entirely on its own. His unit could mobilise and be operational within 30 minutes, he told me, and it was trained not only in normal infantry skills but also in road and bridge demolition, and in the laying of mines. 'We might be heavily outnumbered', he said 'but our fighting spirit would be second to none.'

Illegal crossings of the border into Russia are virtually non-existent. In 1965 an American student called Mott went across: he died later whilst in custody. Recently a Norwegian classed as a mental case strayed across: the Norwegians alerted the Soviet Border Guards who telephoned two days later to say they had picked him up and he was returned. A Norwegian fisherman's boat engine can fail, for instance, bringing him involuntarily into the Soviet river bank. The main border transgressors, however, — and even their crossings are rare — are herds of Norwegian reindeer to whom borders are non-existent. There are some 5,000 reindeer in the Norwegian border area, but none on the Soviet side. The 20-30 bears in the Kirkenes area are not a problem!

When a reindeer incursion takes place, a meeting has to be arranged, out in what is usually a remote area, between the two Border Commissioners, their interpreters and their assistants — together with the reindeer herders. Everyone will be on snow scooters. The officials will confer, make decisions and then monitor events — probably over a picnic livened up by smoked salmon, reindeer meat and cloudberries. Since the new Soviet laws regarding alcohol, its warming powers will be treated as low key: 'we have to drink it out of tea cups now' is one of the current jokes. In the meanwhile the herders will be rounding up their charges and driving them back into Norwegian territory.

Failing such urgently arranged meetings to deal with the unexpected, the Border Commissioners meet regularly once or twice a month on an official basis alternately at each other's Border Conference Houses. The Norwegian one at Storskog — about 100 yards back from the border line — is a simple building centred around an average living room sized conference room. This contains just a wooden table with chairs set along each side, on the top of which stand small Norwegian and Soviet flags. Leading off the room is a small office for the Border Commissioner containing a red telephone which connects him directly with his opposite number on the Soviet side.

Since no Soviet citizen is allowed to approach the controlled border area, illegal crossings into Norway just do not happen. Were such a thing ever to occur, however, as one Soviet Border Commissioner explained recently, he would instantly lose his job and his career would be virtually at an end. Occasionally a few Russian farm pigs may inadvertently stray across, but that is virtually the only sort of incursion that ever takes place from the Soviet side.

It is arguable, however, whether any of the Soviet citizens working there would actually wish to defect from the Kola area, because the whole environment and also the make-up of the population is rather unique.

Over recent years it has been deliberate Soviet policy to create a substantial population in the Kola Peninsula in order to give it roots and stability, and to be the means by which to develop and exploit the area's large natural resources of valuable strategic minerals. Thirty-five percent of the whole of the Soviet Union's consumable salt water fish comes in through Murmansk. A large population also produces a valuable reserve of local manpower

NDN—F

which can be mobilised for defence purposes in case of a national emergency, or even a renewed invasion of the Kola.

The result is that the Kola's population is now more than 1.2 million, whilst that of Murmansk alone is 500,000. The possibilities and potentialities of the region have naturally attracted a youthful working population — 'we do not have any old people' the Kolans say — plus the fact that those who move to the Kola to work are rewarded by very substantial social privileges.

First of all, workers in the Kola are permitted far better and larger houses than they would qualify for in the rest of the Soviet Union. Second, their pay can more than double from around 190 roubles a month to 400. Third, they earn double the normally allowed holidays, being given up to 44 days a year. fourth, they retire at 55, five years earlier than is normal elsewhere. Fifth, and perhaps the most valued privilege, after working in the Kola for 15 years they earn the right to settle anywhere in the Soviet Union, with the sole exception of Moscow.

The infrastructure of the region has been well developed, and schools and hospitals, for instance, are of as high a standard as anywhere else in the country. The Norwegian Border Commissioner told me that on one of his recent visits across the border, accompanied by his Russian colleague, he was taken to a school in a small town of some 350 inhabitants. It has a headmaster and 11 teachers for its 71 pupils. He found the children very alert and well turned out. There was a language laboratory, and obviously the memory and spirit of the 'Great Patriotic War' — the Russian name for World War II — was being kept very much alive amongst the boys and girls.

On the Soviet side, two major factors dominate any thoughts about the border. First, it is never forgotten that two German divisions commanded by General Dietl launched an invasion into Russia across the border from Kirkenes on 29 June 1941 with the object of capturing Murmansk. Thanks to a one week delay in the attack in order to coordinate with the Finns, there was time in which to mobilise every available Soviet citizen in the area and give him a weapon. After very hard fighting under appalling conditions, the German attack was held and defeated on the line of the river Litsa, some 30 miles (50 kilometres) inside the Kola Peninsula.

Following the Russian-Finnish armistice of September 1944, the Soviet Army launched a counter-offensive against the Germans. After more than 300 air strikes on Kirkenes, only 27 houses there were left intact. Capturing the town on 25 October, the Soviet troops pursued the retreating German forces back as far as the Tana River, some 50 miles (80 kilometres) further west. Subsequent urgent demands for manpower from the Central European Front soon reduced the Russian's strength in Northern Norway, until only one battalion was left as the garrison on Kirkenes. This unit was finally withdrawn back across the border into the Kola on 25 September 1945.

In modern German military history the Litsa Valley is now referred to as 'The Valley of Death'; the Soviet Army calls it 'The Valley of Glory'. The well-remembered lesson is that such an enemy build-up and offensive against the Soviet Union's most northerly territory must never be allowed to happen again.

The second dominant factor is the sobering reality that NATO territory so closely adjoins the most sensitive strategic area the Soviet Union possesses. Not only is the border so geographically close on the ground, but the vital bases are also vulnerable to NATO surveillance.

The extensive Soviet military development of the Kola Peninsula in recent years is thus very understandable, and derives from two principal requirements. First is that of the sheer defence of the many vital bases of all Services now located in the region. Second is the need to exploit the potential of the Kola's geographical position as a huge mounting base from which, in time of hostilities, to dominate the Norwegian sea and also to capture Northern Norway's few airfields and ports before NATO can reach them with timely air and ground reinforcements and use them for air attacks on the Kola or Soviet forces.

AT THE ELVENES FRONTIER POST

Henry van Loon

IN the northernmost part of Norway, the South Varanger district of the county of Finnmark, the country shares a 196 kilometre stretch of frontier with the Soviet Union. And an unusual frontier it is, at least to anyone accustomed to the virtually unapproachable Turkish-Russian frontier at Sarp, the shameful Iron Curtain along the border between the two Germanies or the grim crossing-point in Berlin at Checkpoint Charlie. The images which immediately spring to mind in connection with a frontier post with the Soviet Union do not apply here. Some of the Norwegians to whom I spoke about it referred to it as the 'forgotten frontier', others as the 'peaceful frontier' and the frontier commissioner as the 'undramatic frontier'. One Norwegian soldier casually called it a 'friendly frontier'.

On the Norwegian side, there are no restrictions whatever: you can fly to Kirkenes by Twin Otter and then drive the 5 kilometres to the frontier without any difficulty. There are no road-blocks, no soldiers; road No. 886, which runs to the border, does have a number of warning signs, but all they say is 'Beware of skiers'. Right next to the actual frontier post are notices in three languages pointing out that the Soviet Union starts here and that the photographing of Soviet territory is not permitted — no more in fact than 'shaking a fist towards the other side or making threatening gestures'. Even that seems unlikely, because as far as the eye can see, not a soul is visible on the Russian side. On the Norwegian side, runs a lightweight medium-height fence; on the Soviet side, the fences are heavier and higher. There is a no man's land with no mines but with sensors which sound an alarm should anyone stray too close to the fences. Frontier commissioner Inge A. Torhaug says: 'There's more point in that than you might think — our fence serves to stop reindeer, theirs to stop people.' He tells how his Soviet opposite number candidly admits that his only major concern is that a Russian defector might try to escape over the frontier to the West. At an informal meeting the Russian told Torhaug: 'My main job here is to prevent Soviet citizens from fleeing the country. No one in Moscow cares about what I'm doing here, but if anyone were to cross the frontier here to the West illegally that would be the end of my career — and bang would go any chance of promotion!'

Incidents occur, but only rarely — and none at all on the Soviet side, simply because no Soviet citizen is permitted to come anywhere near the frontier. The day before I arrived there had been such a 'border incident': a herd of Norwegian reindeer had broken through the fence and were grazing on the Soviet side. In the midst of the wilderness a meeting then had to be arranged between the two frontier commissioners, their interpreters and the herdsmen in question, who went off on their snow scooters as soon as they had received authorization to round up the animals and drive them back on to Norwegian territory. The officials killed time with an impromptu picnic in the snow and many a toast to the success of the enterprise.

Torhaug continued: 'When party leader Gorbachev began his campaign against alcoholism in the Soviet Union, my Soviet opposite number remarked jokingly: "Today we must drink an extra dram — because tomorrow we won't be allowed to anymore".'

In spite of the apparent joviality, the contrast between the guard kept on the two sides of the frontier is striking. The Norwegian frontier force consists of 150 men, 7 frontier posts and about 10 unobtrusive look-out towers, known as 'observation posts', from which, according to the letter of the agreement, the Norwegians may not take any photographs of Soviet territory.

The Norwegian frontier company, which forms part of the 500-strong South Varanger garrison from Kirkenes, is made up of the cream of the Norwegian conscript forces. As the garrison commanding officer, Lieutenant-Colonel Ola Petter Løvlien, says: 'They are all conscripts, but as volunteers they are individually hand-picked for intelligence, conduct, physical fitness, etc. In every respect they must be the best soldiers in the Norwegian conscript army, and if they are not up to the mark they are irrevocably removed from the frontier service and returned to their original garrisons'. Although most of the soldiers from the South Varanger area come from the Oslo region (2,500 km farther south), not a single one of this select band would willingly do anything else. They are conscious of their own worth, and feel that they are an élite group within the Norwegian army. They admit that 'there is always something interesting to do here; you simply don't have time to get bored.' Routine patrols, which they carry out in summer in temperatures of up to +30 degrees Centigrade and in winter in temperatures of down to -45 degrees, may last 10 hours and cover *several hundred kilometres, some of it on foot, some by bicycle, on skis, by snow scooter, tracked vehicle, motor boat or helicopter.*

In their wooden huts it is noticeable how their personal weapons and live ammunition are kept within close reach. Next to the door in racks are the short AG-3 rifles and Carl Gustav anti-tank weapons. The heaviest weapon with which the garrison is equipped is the TOW. There are no tanks, anti-aircraft artillery or heavy guns here. The Norwegians know that if they are attacked there is little they can do other than make life difficult for the invaders by guerrilla tactics, while withdrawing to the first resistance zone near Tromsö, 800 kilometres away.

On the Soviet side, the picture is completely different: 850-strong KGB troops are responsible for maintaining the frontier guard (enjoying all kinds of privileges such as long leaves and early retirement). As a back-up they have 2 motorized infantry divisions and a marine infantry brigade — and it is assumed at least 2 Spetsnaz brigades and support units. Within 150 kilometres of the frontier lies Murmansk at the heart of the Kola Peninsula, where no fewer than 350,000 Soviet troops are stationed — in what is undoubtedly one of the densest military zones of the world.

Nevertheless, the enormous Soviet military might so close to their northern frontier is not the subject of daily conversation among the Norwegian soldiers. 'We know they're there. We see them and they see us — but they behave quite normally. You have to go back as far as 1968 for any kind of minor incident here. Allied exercises were under way in the Tromsö region when one day no fewer than 400 Soviet tanks came rolling right up to the frontier, all of them with their guns trained on Norwegian territory. That was certainly no joke, but even then everything turned out all right.'

Not for nothing, after all, is this called the peaceful frontier.

Baltic Strategy Past and Present

ROLF HALLERBACH

What the Russians refer to as 'Baltiyskoye' is known by the Poles as 'Morze Baltyckie' and by the Finns as 'Itameri'. In Swedish it is called 'Osterskon' and in German 'Ostsee'. All mean the same: the Baltic Sea. This 420,000 square kilometres area of water both divides and unites the European mainland and the Scandinavian peninsula. As an inland sea with a few narrow exits to the world's oceans, the Baltic has, throughout history, tempted strategically-minded political and military leaders to control the approaches and exits, and thus hold sway over the Baltic states.

Between about 700 and 1000 AD, the Danish and Swedish Vikings used the Baltic to conduct a flourishing trade which extended beyond its eastern shores into Slav and Finnish territory. In the 11th century, the Slavs took over the Baltic trade and, a century later, German merchants joined together to form a Baltic economic area. In 1161 the latter founded the Hanseatic League with remarkably modern forms of economic warfare such as subsidies and boycotts to consolidate its grip on Baltic trade. The Hanseatic League came into conflict with Danish attempts to unify Scandinavia and create a great Baltic state. In 1429 Erik, Duke of Pomerania, crowned King of Denmark, Norway and Sweden over 30 years earlier, felt strong enough to force users of the Baltic entrances to pay him Sound Dues. Denmark continued to levy these tolls until 1857 and still claims the right to control the passage of warships through the Baltic entrances. Erik's ambitions crumbled, however, thanks in part to Hanseatic pressure. Power in the Baltic remained divided between Denmark, Sweden, Poland and the rising stars of Russia and Brandenburg-Prussia.

As empires rose and fell, the Baltic peoples grew familiar with foreign rule. By 1815 all the Baltic's eastern shores from Tornio to Memel had come into the Russian Empire. Prussia, the core of the later German Empire,

PLATE 16. Eric of Pomerania, King of Denmark, Norway and Sweden.
(*Royal Library, Copenhagen*)

controlled the southern shores from Memel to Schleswig-Holstein (which German province Prussia finally took from Denmark in the 1860s). After the Russian Revolution of 1917 and in the turbulent period following the end of the First World War, the peoples of the eastern and south eastern Baltic shores made a bid for national independence. Finland, Estonia, Latvia and Lithuania carved themselves out of pre-war Russia. Newly independent Poland thrust a corridor to the sea at the expense of Germany. Both old masters planned to restore the situation. Germany and Russia jointly invaded Poland in 1939, and in 1940 the three Baltic states, with a total population of over 6,000,000 people and covering an area of 117,000 square kilometres were annexed by the Soviet Union. Finland provided a tougher nut to crack, but had to give up territory between Lake Ladoga and the Gulf of Finland. At the end of World War II, the Soviet Union greatly improved its strategic position in the Baltic. By massive annexations stretching into old East Prussia, its domination of Poland and its occupation of a zone of Germany, the USSR increased the area of Baltic shore under its control from a mere 200 kilometres to 2500. Since then, the USSR has retained and built up shipyards and port facilities in the Baltic. Not only do these facilities form an important line of communication westwards, one that is increasing in importance (see box), but they are still vital support facilities for the Soviet fleets. Bearing in mind that about half the Soviets' total European naval dockyard capacity is on the Baltic coast, the extent of this dependence becomes clear.

A NEW GATEWAY TO THE BALTIC

The Soviet Union and East Germany have reduced the distance that separates them through the realisation of a huge and costly transport project. Since October 1986, a ferry service links the Soviet coastal town of Memel (renamed Klaipéda) to Mukran on Rugen Island, located a few miles away from the East German coastline.

Heinz Rentner, Transport Minister of the GDR, described this sealink as a new 'gateway to the Baltic', which should bring to an end the difficulties of transporting Soviet goods by rail through Polish territory. The two harbours are no more than 273 miles (500 kilometres) apart.

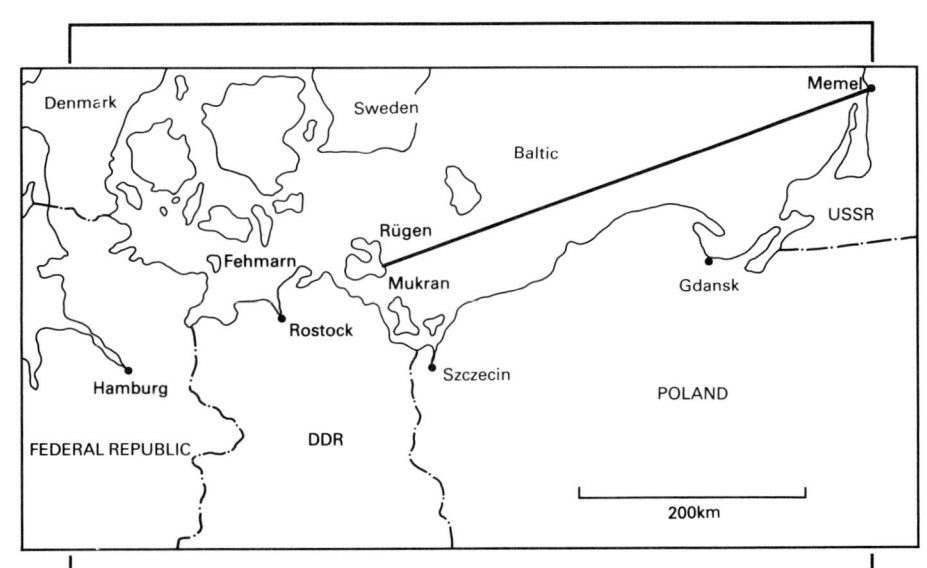

MAP 9. The Memel – Mukran Ferry.

The small town of Mukran, a fishing port until only a few years ago has undergone radical transformation. The population was resettled elsewhere to make space for 1,000 new apartments built to accommodate railway and dock workers. In the meantime, Mukran has turned into a lively port city used for international maritime traffic. 2.8 million cubic metres of sand have been removed to facilitate access to the port and allow the docking of large ships, and a 200 metre long pier has been built. The harbour has 60 kilometres of railway track of which 20 kilometres are the broad gauge used in the Soviet Union. The 'Mukran' a large car ferry and the first in a series of six other ships on the production line, is to assure a regular maritime link between the two ports. It is 190 metres long, 28 metres wide and carries 11,700 tons of goods at a speed averaging 30 kilometres per hour.

The shipyard Matthias-Thesen in Wismar (East Germany) is due to build three more ships for the GDR and three for the Soviet Union by 1989. Each car ferry has two decks providing sufficient space for

> *approximately 103 wide-gauge Soviet railway waggons. Once construction work has been completed, a ship should be able to dock in Mukran and Klaipéda every 8 hours. It is anticipated that the yearly exchange of goods will reach 5.3 million tons by 1990.*
>
> *This impressive project has brought to an end what officials in both countries regarded as the 'Polish problem'. Goods transported by rail via Poland were often plundered and badly handled by Polish workers. The sealink not only offers obvious commercial advantages for the two countries but also enables Moscow to gain access to a huge harbour located close to the West which could also be used for military purposes. Rügen and the West German Baltic Island Fehmarn are only 120 kilometres apart. The Danish Island of Falster lies only 75 kilometres away from Rügen.*

Admiral Gorshkov, the man whom many regard as primarily responsible for creating the modern Soviet fleet, gave a coded signal when he was asked about the build-up in the Baltic. The Admiral put it very succinctly by replying: 'The Baltic is just a swimming pool'. This memorable answer underlined the fact that he was not just talking about the Baltic but about access to the Atlantic.

The Allied Command tasked with preventing that access is NATO Headquarters Baltic Approaches — abbreviated in Alliance terminology as BALTAP. Led by a Danish commander, with a German deputy and a Danish/German/British/American staff, BALTAP is responsible for the defence of Denmark, Schleswig-Holstein and Hamburg north of the Elbe. The officers at Headquarters BALTAP see the Baltic Approaches as part of the strategic triangle which they form together with Northern Norway and Iceland. Because of their proximity to central Europe and the Warsaw Pact, the Baltic Approaches have assumed a special role within this triangle. Extending from the southern tip of Norway, via the Danish islands, Jutland and Schleswig-Holstein to the border between the two Germanies and the Elbe, they are part of NATO territory. This means that they are in our hands and are defended by our own forces. Preparations can thus already be made for their defence in peacetime.

From this situation, which is favourable to the Alliance, two things follow. First, possession of the Baltic Approaches is a *sine qua non* for the cohesion of NATO defence in Europe. Secondly, in view of their paramount strategic importance for NATO and the Warsaw Pact commanders, the Baltic Approaches are an area where it is likely that, in the event of a conflict, there would be extremely intensive action.

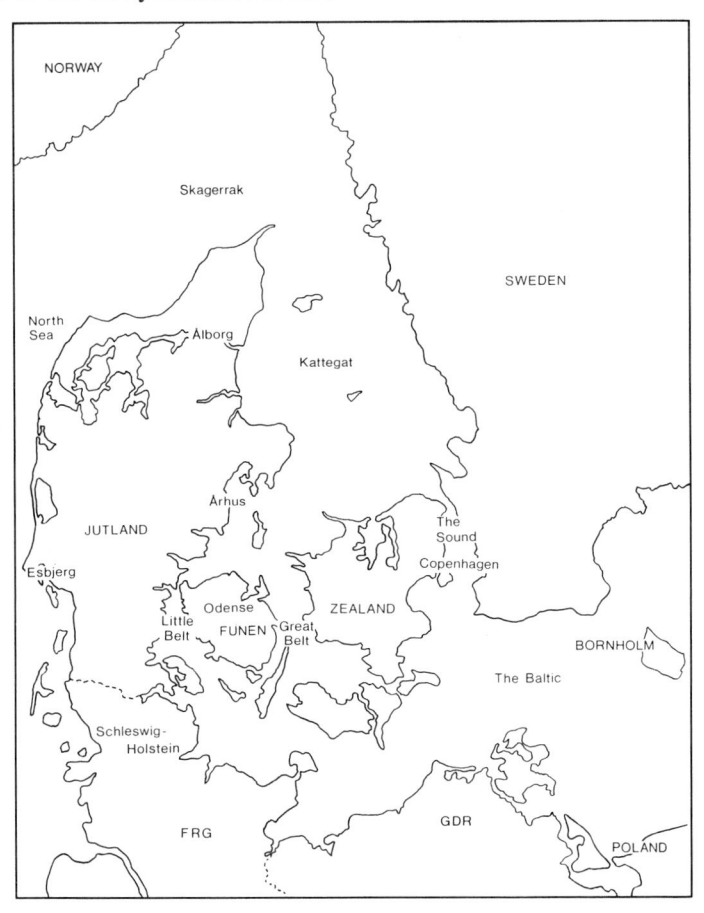

MAP 10. Denmark and the Baltic Approaches. Denmark consists of some 400 islands and more than 7000 kilometres of coastline.

Moscow appears to want to take advantage of this situation by playing upon the fears of the population. Both Denmark and Norway, whose solidarity with NATO is being undermined by the seductive idea of a nuclear-free zone in Northern Europe, are priority targets for Soviet propaganda. However, such ideas and the promise of peace which they hold out, immediately lose their attractiveness when it is seen how categorically the Soviets reject the notion of including their own territory, for instance, around Murmansk, in a nuclear-free zone.

Doubts about the peaceful intentions of the Soviet Union are also raised and increasingly fuelled by the activities of Soviet submarines in the neutral waters of Sweden.

PLATE 17. Part of the amphibious threat in the Baltic: an AIST class landing hovercraft. (*Danish Defence*)

In the 50s and 60s Warsaw Pact manoeuvres centred on the eastern Baltic, but since the 70s the exercises, such as 'Comrades in Arms 1986', have also demonstrated the ability of the Warsaw Pact forces to make combined attacks involving air, land and sea forces and conduct landings in the western Baltic. NATO keeps a very close watch on the activities of the

PLATE 18. A Soviet *Tarantul* class fast attack craft in Oresund.   (*Danish Defence*)

Eastern bloc's armed forces. For this purpose, the radar installations on the Danish island of Bornholm provide it with an ideal observation post. This island, known as 'NATO's eye in the Baltic', is situated some 200 kilometres east of the Iron Curtain, and from this vantage point it is possible to look deep into the flank and the backyard of a number of Warsaw Pact states and also into the territory of the Soviet Union itself. Indeed, it remains Moscow's secret why, after the War in 1946, it handed back to Denmark this strategically important island. (See following chapter — 'The Bornholm Story'.)

The surveillance of the two blocs which face each other in the Baltic is a two-way affair. Thus, after a long Atlantic crossing, Soviet warships drop anchor off the North eastern coast of Jutland to take on board fresh supplies. Three observation vessels — one from Poland, one East German and one from the Soviet Union — lie out of the Danish islands year in, year out. However, because that is not enough, the Soviets have placed another vessel north of the Great Belt. The systematic surveillance of the straits is augmented by regular sailings by East German and Polish ships around the main island of Sjaelland. The air force is not inactive either. Operating from bases in the Soviet Union, sometimes as many as 50 aircraft fly provocatively close to the Danish border and conduct simulated bombing raids.

All this, in the opinion of senior NATO officers at BALTAP Headquarters in Karup, is of only superficial relevance in military terms. There are more important factors affecting the delicate equilibrium of the 'Nordic Balance' in the Baltic. If Denmark, for instance, were to dilute further its contribution to the Alliance, this would immediately have a destabilising effect. Such fears are not pure fantasy. This was made clear by Knud Damgaard, the Danish Social Democrats' defence expert, in a conversation with journalists. Fully aware of the major role played by his Party in Denmark, he set out his view as follows: the situation in the Baltic is not dangerous; NATO's analysis of the 'threat' and its comparison of the armed forces are exaggerated; the Danish Navy is now no longer capable of aggressive action but this still does not go far enough. Frigates and submarines are superfluous. Landing units can be dealt with more effectively and, above all, more cheaply, with land based missiles. For Mr.

PLATE 19. Mining is crucial to blocking the Baltic exits.　　(*Danish Defence*)

Damgaard and those who share his views, all this has nothing to do with a lack of will to defend the country; there is still the Danish Home Guard. It is, however, doubtful whether the Home Guard exerts the deterrent effect on the Soviets required by NATO strategy. Submarines, for example, are crucial instruments of defensive ASW.

ASW IN THE BALTIC

Jules J. Vaessen

THE BALTIC *is a shallow, non-tidal sea. A number of rivers discharge their water into it, turning the sea brackish. Large parts freeze over in the Winter, only to melt again in Spring and early Summer. To the submariners' delight and the chagrin of ASW operators, these two phenomena create solid and impenetrable layers. In an effort to find ASW systems that can operate under the layers, maritime aircraft, helicopters and submarines are used. Maritime aircraft use sonobuoys with long cables to which hydrophones are connected. The length of cable is adjusted to allow search under the layers. Helicopters hover and lower their sonar transducers on cables down to the appropriate depth. Best suited of all is the submarine. It simply measures temperature and salinity as it submerges until it finds the optimum depth, where it lies in wait for its prey.*

The result is cause for concern. If the Danes significantly reduce their capacity for forward defence in the Baltic, the Germans will have to bear more of the burden. East of Bornholm, the Federal German Navy currently deploys Tornado missile-firing fighter-bombers, of which there will be over 100 by the mid 1990s, and 18 class 206/206A submarines. The latter are difficult to track. They can also lay mines.

West of Bornholm (see next Chapter), a wide array of instruments of naval warfare are deployed, including, in addition to fighter bombers, fast attack craft and combat helicopters, and also a new generation of mines which do not restrict one's own operational freedom and take only a short time to lay.

The German Navy is not deployed merely to safeguard the exits from the Baltic and for combat duty in the Baltic. It also provides a contingent outside the Baltic which helps to safeguard the Northern Flank generally. The Bundesmarine is involved in forward defence and escort duties in the North Sea and North Atlantic with 16 major combat vessels, 6 submarines and 19 submarine-hunter aircraft. Of the 16 combat vessels, six are 3,600 Bremen class missile frigates each carrying two helicopters. Two more of this class are due in 1989-90. By 1995 the Navy will have available 30 tenders and supply ships for supporting all vessels in the North Sea, the Baltic and neighbouring waters.

Weapons alone, however, cannot replace the political will to assert and defend oneself. If the forces of one individual within an Alliance are insufficient this does not mean that the Alliance is defenceless. Solidarity is its strength. It must be demonstrated, if the leadership in Moscow is to understand that peace and security will be energetically defended throughout NATO territory. Can we really believe, however, that the message is getting through?

PLATE 20. One of Denmark's vital submarines. (*Danish Defence*)

On the endangered Northern Flank of the Alliance there is no multi-national presence in peacetime. Until recently, some Canadian reinforcements were designated for the area but this commitment has now been withdrawn. The Canadian Government has announced its intention to redirect the Canadian commitment to reinforce Allied Command Europe from the Northern to Central Region. Would there not be something to be gained from a multi-national presence in Schleswig-Holstein?

Despite the unquestionable need to plan carefully the defence of certain regions, including of course the Baltic, we should never forget that the fate of Europe will be decided first and foremost in the Atlantic. Secure sea links between North America and Europe are the essential prerequisite for the defence of Europe. Defending the seas on the edge of the Atlantic will bar the way to Soviet fleets and prevent them from disrupting those links. Although the Baltic may be 'just a swimming pool' it is not one reserved for the exclusive use of the Soviets. As long as the West is able to control access to this 'pool', its freedom in the Atlantic will not be endangered.

The Bornholm Story

ROLF HALLERBACH

AT THE end of the war, hardly anyone dared think that Bornholm, the Danish island 150 miles east of the Iron Curtain, would be able to live outside the Soviet sphere of influence. Soviet bomber squadrons had severely damaged parts of the two main towns, Nekso and Ronne, and Soviet troops had moved in to occupy the island. All this was going on while the rest of Denmark was celebrating its liberation. On 4th May 1945 Admiral Georg von Friedeburg had signed the documents of surrender of the German armed forces at Montgomery's headquarters in Luneburg. The Commandant of Bornholm at that time, Captain Gert von Kamptz, who is now in his eighties and lives in retirement in Kiel, clearly remembers those last dramatic days of the war:

> 'On 6 May 1945 the radio message was received reporting the surrender of the German Armed Forces in Holland, Northern Germany and Denmark. I immediately ordered a ceasefire and made arrangements for handing over the island to the British, but they did not come. Instead, a Russian ultimatum arrived, but no reply was given. There followed Russian air raids on Nekso and Ronne, which I thought would be in preparation for a Russian landing. I was resolved to repulse any such attacks, in order to safeguard the transport of refugees through the Baltic for as long as possible.'

Bornholm commands the channel through the Baltic and was, therefore, the last link with the West for the German troops cut off in Kurland and East Prussia. Bornholm was also the last escape route for refugees from the East. After the evacuation of the Ninth Army from East Poland, which took place between 4th and 6th May, there were more than 22,000 soldiers and several thousand refugees on the island, hoping to escape the Soviets.

Aware of this situation, Captain von Kamptz refused to surrender. He held fast even when the Soviets bombed Nekso and Ronne for the first time on 7 May. He told the regional Commander of the Danish resistance movement, who since 4 May had been operating openly, that he did not intend, as demanded by the Soviets, to turn up at 10.00 hours at the port of Kotobrzeg to negotiate the terms of the surrender. In his letter of 8 May 1945, he wrote:

'The German forces on Bornholm have orders to protect the island against any attack. Under the terms of the armistice, Bornholm is a British sphere of influence. I have orders to let only the British land on Bornholm.'

Only about 10 percent of all the houses survived the bombing by two Soviet squadrons which took place on the morning of 8 May. With great foresight, both towns had been completely evacuated the night before, so there were no victims among the population. From numerous interrogations during his nine years in captivity, Captain von Kamptz was amazed to discover that the Russian leaders had been under the impression that the British had already occupied Bornholm on 5 May, so that, with the

PLATE 21. Soviet troops in devastated Bornholm. (*Museet for Danmarks Frihedskamp 1940-1945*)

Germans, they could defend the island against Russian attacks. 'Thus', he concluded, 'the Russian attacks would not only have been directed against the German occupation of the island.'

On 8 May the island Commandant received a radio message instructing him to surrender unconditionally. This included surrendering to the Russians:

'Now I saw that my job had come to an end. I handed my command over to General Wuthmann, who had come from East Prussia. I asked him to conduct all the negotiations relating to the handing over of the island. We still hoped, however, that the British would arrive before the Russians.'

This hope was to prove false. On 9 May, Armistice Day, when many people lost their lives in Soviet attacks on German convoys off Christianso, due northeast of Bornholm, Soviet forces in speedboats landed on the island. The German occupying forces and all the refugees were taken prisoner.

Captain von Kamptz's verdict is quite categoric:

> 'The German occupation of Bornholm helped make it possible for over two million refugees and wounded to be transported by sea from East to West. After 5 May 1945 alone, over 50,000 more people were brought to safety to the West.'

The inhabitants of Bornholm put up with the Soviet occupation in the same way as they had put up with the German occupation, with calmness and equanimity. Far back in the island's history, when the Swedes had taken and occupied Bornholm in 1658, it had been a different story Then, the inhabitants of the island killed the Swedish Commandant and cast off the yoke of oppression.

The situation was now very different. The German occupation on 10 April 1940 had passed off peacefully. The infantry battalion deployed as the first unit on the island was very soon required elsewhere and replaced by a company of 'remarkably old soldiers', as they were described in a report at the time. These too were withdrawn and the island came under the administration of the Navy. Arrangements were made to install 38 centimetre (15-inch) guns at Dueodde, on the southern tip of the island, to command the passage south of Bornholm in conjunction with the batteries on the German coast. At the last minute, the German Armed Forces required the guns elsewhere and this plan came to nothing. Bornholm thus remained just a staging post and was largely unfortified.

The inhabitants of the island were nevertheless puzzled about the purpose of the electronic surveillance installations built by the German Navy. Colonel Heiberg-Jurgensen, the present head of the military district of Bornholm, remembers the day when the puzzle was solved:

> 'In August 1943, an unmanned aircraft had landed intact on the island. Such objects had already been sighted a number of times, but on this occasion two officers of the Danish Resistance managed to take photographs and make sketches before German soldiers were able to seal off the place where it had landed. This information was secretly taken to Sweden by fishermen and from there reached London. The V-1 had been discovered and the cover of Peenemunde as their secret testing ground had been blown.'

PLATE 22. Another view of the Soviet occupation of Bornholm. (*Museet for Danmarks Frihedskamp 1940–1945*)

At the beginning of March 1946, ten months after the occupation of Bornholm by the Russians, the Danish Ambassador in Moscow handed over a note from his Government stating that the Danish Government was again in a position to guarantee the security of the island with its own armed forces. The presence of the Soviets was therefore no longer necessary. They were asked, as the British had already been asked, to withdraw their troops completely from Denmark. Moscow's reply read as follows:

> 'As soon as Denmark is in a position to occupy and administer Bornholm without the participation of foreign troops, the Soviet Union will withdraw its troops and hand Bornholm back to Denmark.'

The Danes reacted swiftly. On 8 March, the Danish Foreign Minister informed the Russian Ambassador in Copenhagen that the time had come to hand back Bornholm, as Denmark was now able to take over sole responsibility for the protection and administration of the island. On 5 April 1946, Moscow withdrew the last of its 8,000 soldiers. 'The feeling on Bornholm was that we had got off lightly once again,' was how Colonel Heiberg-Jurgensen described that day.

In view of the dearth of historical documents, there is scope for considerable speculation as to why the Soviets let the island go. Today, one thing is for certain, though — they regret having done so.

Enough Deterrence to Deter?

ERICH HAUSER

WHEN Denmark and Norway became founding members of NATO in 1949, both their governments declared that no allied troops and no atomic weapons were to be stationed on their territory in peacetime. This formula has been upheld ever since without any obvious detriment to deterrence.

Part of the political reasoning behind this doctrine was, and remains, the so-called 'Nordic Balance' which has to take account both of Sweden's neutrality and of Finland, which has a special relationship with the Soviet Union but nevertheless remains a neutral country. The theory of 'Nordic Balance' implies that any change on one side would more or less automatically bring about changes on the other side. Indeed, changes have occurred. Over the past two decades, the Kola Peninsula has become the most important base for the Soviet Navy and for Moscow's strategic missile submarines. It is an area criss-crossed with a dense network of military installations of all kinds, described in more detail in other chapters of this book. In the Baltic, the Soviet Union and its Warsaw Pact partners have increased their amphibious landing capability intended for use in the Baltic Approaches, in combination with their air attack squadrons.

These developments only serve to underline the strategic importance of Norway and Denmark in the case of a conflict. Both countries have, therefore, felt the need, together with their Alliance partners, to improve and extend existing reinforcement plans for times of crisis, to increase the frequency and scope of reinforcement exercises and to implement plans to pre-position stocks of arms and equipment in order to ensure rapid combat readiness of Allied reinforcements if they were ever needed.

None of these developments, however, have changed the general public perception of the Nordic Area as a region of relatively low tension, an image that all Scandinavian governments as well as Moscow seem eager to uphold. These efforts were only slightly disturbed by the famous 'whisky-on-the-

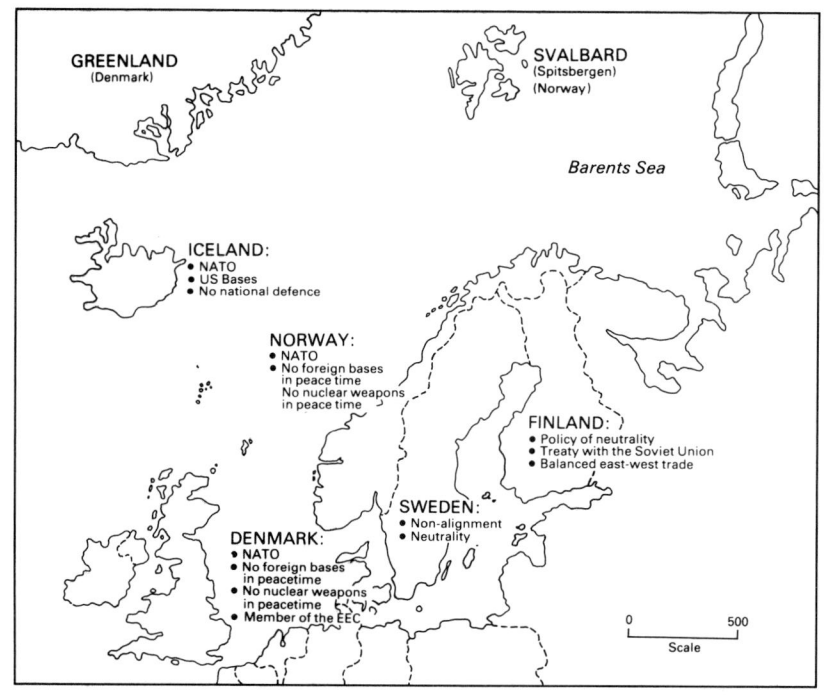

MAP 11. The Nordic Balance.

rocks' incident, when a Soviet submarine was stranded near Sweden's naval base Karskona; or by the spy case involving the Norwegian government official, Arne Treholt, which highlighted the tough superpower attitude demonstrated by the Soviets towards Oslo in the dispute about economic and fishing rights in the Barents Sea. After each of these incidents the respective Governments of Sweden and Norway not only refrained from stirring up the public outcry but did their best to play it down.

Are Scandinavian governments indulging in appeasement policy? That view is widely held in some circles in the United States, but it is quite wrong. Since the 'whisky-on-the-rocks' incident, Sweden has increased its efforts to patrol its long and difficult coastal waters more effectively. More important for NATO, and no doubt to the great relief of Alliance defence planners, Stockholm has significantly stepped up defence precautions and defence

PLATE 23. Fast attack craft form a basic element in the naval dimension of the Nordic balance. This is *Bredal* one of the ten torpedo/missile boats of the Danish *Willemoes* class.   (*Danish Defence*)

plans for Northern Sweden over the past 10 years or so. (For Sweden's posture see the box.) The danger of Soviet forces being able to pass through neutral Sweden comparatively easily in order to attack Northern Norway seems to have diminished. But part of the co-operative policy espoused by the four Scandinavian governments is to avoid any mention in public of contacts and exchange of ideas — clandestine or otherwise – between military and political defence experts of the two neutral and the two NATO countries.

ARMED NEUTRALITY

Swedish foreign and defence policy is aimed at maintaining armed neutrality in case of a conflict in the area. Swedish territory is not considered to give NATO or the Warsaw Pact strategic advantages in a conflict, but it may be used to gain access to important areas in the North and to open the Baltic exits.

Sweden has a strong defence, which to a large extent is based on general conscription and mobilization. The peacetime land forces consist of a number of regiments (equivalents) which conduct both basic and refresher training, and which parts of the year may fill readiness functions. In the Upper Norrland Military District such units include I22 in Kiruna, I19 in Boden and K4 (Jaeger battalion) in Arvidsjaur on the highway to Norway (Graddisvegen).

In recent years, Sweden has strengthened its defence in North Sweden by establishing another Norrland brigade and by improving the conditions for quick transfer of brigades from Central and South Sweden. Upon mobilization Sweden will activate:

Field Army:
Divisional headquarters with staff and signal units.
About 100 independent infantry, jaeger, armoured, infantry and AA (missile) battalions
10 infantry brigades, type 77
8 infantry brigades, type 66M
5 Norrland brigades
4 armoured brigades
1 mechanized brigade
A total of about 300,000 men.

Coastal Artillery
Coastal artillery brigades
Barrier battalions and companies
Coastal artillery battalions
Minelaying divisions
Coastal jaeger companies
Artillery and missile batteries
Command and supply units
A total of about 60 units.

> **Local Defence**
> *About 90 battalions*
> *About 400 independent companies*
> *A total of about 300,000 men.*
> **The Home Guard:** *120,000 men.*
> **Total Army:** *about 700,000 men.*
> **Navy:**
> *12 submarines*
> *2 coastal corvettes*
> *16 torpedo/missile vessels*
> *16 patrol boats*
> *3 mining vessels and auxiliary vessels*
> *Minesweepers*
> *Helicopters*
> *Command and base units.*
>
> **Air Force:**
> *11 fighter squadrons (about 220 aircraft)*
> *5½ medium attack squadrons and*
> *4 light attack squadrons (about 150 aircraft)*
> *6 reconnaissance squadrons (about 55 aircraft)*
> *1 transport squadron and 5 transport aircraft groups*
> *5 communications air groups*
> *5 scout plane units*
> *10 helicopter groups*
> *44 base and combat control battalions*
> *Air surveillance battalions*
>
> The Swedish Armed Forces consist of some 850,000 men, including the Home Guard. In war they will be concentrated in three main areas: Upper Norrland, Central Sweden with Stockholm, and South Sweden.
>
> (Source: The Military Balance in Northern Europe 1987-1988 pages 20-21, prepared by the Norwegian Atlantic Committee and based upon The Military Balance 1987-1988 published by the International Institute of Strategic Studies, London.)

It was more than twenty years ago that the late President of Finland, Urho Kekkonen, proposed to make the whole of Scandinavia a 'nuclear free zone'. The idea has, of course, been kept alive by Moscow, by left wing movements and also by the late Swedish Social Democrat leader, Olaf Palme. He, however, realised the practical impossibility of creating such a zone in the North without extending it to Central Europe; and that, of course, remains equally unrealistic without fundamental changes in the military postures of both NATO and the Warsaw Pact to reduce the conventional imbalance of their respective forces.

It is remarkable how steadfastly the governments of Denmark and Norway — whether Conservative or Social Democrat — have refused to let themselves be tempted by the 'nuclear free zone' idea, despite its popular appeal from the beginning, and particularly in the early 80s, in the wake of NATO's famous 'double track decision' of December 1979. Oslo and Copenhagen have stuck to their traditional formula: in peacetime, no atomic weapons and no foreign troops. The nuclear option thereby remains for times when conflict might be imminent. Public opinion in Scandinavia has always been aware that NATO's strategy of 'flexible response' included the two northern members of the Alliance.

However, the seemingly privileged status enjoyed by Denmark and Norway within the Alliance, together with the low-tension image projected from Scandinavia as a whole, has not been without repercussions. It helped to accentuate a general feeling in Western Germany, which went well beyond the active membership of the Peace Movement, generated by the 1979 double-track decision, that the Federal Republic of Germany was singled out for stationing the highest concentration of nuclear warheads anywhere in the world. This, of course, had been a fact since the 50s, as had the similarly singular concentration of Allied troops from seven other NATO nations on a territory roughly one-third smaller than Norway's.

Up until the 70s, in fact, the vast majority of the West German population had willingly accepted these facts as consequences, first of Hitler's war and then of the perceived Soviet threat — an acceptance which was accompanied by a growing feeling of security on the one hand and a growing realisation of the importance of the Bonn Government's role, particularly with regard to East-West *détente*.

It was, therefore, a combined shock to awaken to the fact that not only did the *détente* era appear to have been terminated by the Reagan Administration in Washington, but that the Federal Republic's 'special status' within NATO was as a predestined battlefield in a superpower conflict — the implication being that it faced the prospect of total destruction. The shock was to reach such proportions that in 1982 the German Social Democratic Party fled from its Chancellor Helmut Schmidt and from his policies in an unprecedented mass desertion. This turnabout occurred within months and caused the fall of his Government. Rather to the surprise of the Party, the General Election in January 1983 indicated that the widely spread feeling of anxiety in the population had not been quite as strong as had been believed.

Yet, the rank and file membership of the SPD, with strong pacifist traditions emanating from the First and Second World Wars, showed no readiness at all to return to the concept of the defence policy which had enabled it to participate in government in Bonn without interruption from 1969 to 1982.

The Party leadership, and particularly its many 'security experts', instead chose the path of searching for a new defence concept in close co-operation with the Social Democratic and Socialist Parties of Denmark, Norway, the Netherlands, Belgium and even Sweden. And the repercussions of this, stengthened by parallel developments in the Labour Party of the United Kingdom, appear to be of growing significance in Scandinavia and foremost in Denmark.

In 1987 the Danish 'Folketing' (Parliament) was to decide on the country's next five-year plan for defence acquisitions. Given the strength of political forces, this could not be done without the Danish Social Democratic Party, no matter what coalition of parties was in power. Just as the German SPD, at its Party Convention in Essen in January of 1983, had established the principle that it would make the Federal German Armed Forces *struckturellisch Nichtangriffsfahig* — in other words, transform them

PLATE 24. F-16 fighters form the core striking forces of both the Danish and Norwegian Air Forces. (*Danish Defence*)

into a force incapable of being used for attack, so the Danish Social Democratic Party had decided to aim at a 'defensive defence policy'. It did not matter that not even Communist propaganda had ever dared to attribute aggressive potential to Denmark's armed forces. The idea was first put forward by the left wing Socialist People's Party, which in the past had gained voters to the detriment of the Social Democrats.

In concrete terms, the Danish Social Democratic leader and ex-Prime Minister Anker Jorgensen had already defined his Party's conditions for the new five-year plan by the Autumn of 1986:

- Denmark's F-16 fighter planes should be restricted to air defence, abandoning their dual capability as bombers.
- Denmark's frigates and submarines were not to be modernised or even replaced, because the strategic Danish Straits could just as well be defended if their Harpoon missiles were transferred from the ships to shore positions.
- And finally, the Danish Government, in the context of the new defence plan, should warn its NATO partners that even in times of international crisis, no nuclear weapons would be allowed on Danish soil.

Interestingly enough, it was the then Social Democratic Government of Norway which, immediately after Jorgensen's announcements, demanded explanations from the Conservative coalition Government in Copenhagen rather than from the Danish Social Democrats, Prime Minister Poul Schluter and Foreign Minister Uffe Ellemann-Jensen responded in public that Alliance plans for the reinforcement of Denmark with American and British forces 'could no longer be reckoned with' if they were refused nuclear weapons as a last resort.

NATO being an alliance of sovereign nations, it is clear that the other member countries have to tolerate whatever decision is taken by the Danish Parliament. Danish footnotes to NATO communiqués, imposed upon the Government by a majority on the 'Folketing', have been routine since the double-track decision of 1979 — so much so that NATO Secretary General, Lord Carrington, once quipped at a press conference: 'They are so traditional that we almost tend to forget what they are about.'

It is equally clear that the relative weakness of the Danish defence posture is in stark contrast to its geographical importance in any imaginable conflict in Europe and that this weakness has over the years forced other partners — particularly the Federal Republic of Germany and the United Kingdom —

to carry a greater share of responsibility for the defence of the North. If the Danish Navy were to become virtually non-existent as far as operations in the Baltic Sea are concerned, and lost the capacity to resist approaching amphibious forces of the Warsaw Pact in the early stages of a conflict, it would obviously be a loss of 'deterrence' of proportions which would be intolerable to NATO as a whole. Either the German Navy or British, Dutch and other naval units would have to fill the gap, even in peacetime.

It is interesting that even for a few months before the German Federal election of January 1987, the West German SPD had never clearly spelt out all the necessary details of its concept of *'strukturelle Nichtangriffsfahigkeit'* of the Bundeswehr. Different 'experts' of the Party wrote contradictory papers. And, of course, there was the spectacular 'agreement' between the West German SPD in opposition and the governing East German SED on the plan for a 'nuclear free zone' in Central Europe which would cover 150 kilometres of the border area between the two German states as well as between the Federal Republic and the CSSR.

As the West German state of Schleswig-Holstein on the Jutland Peninsula is little more than 100 kilometres wide and touches the East German border just behind the city of Lubeck, it was obvious that this plan — if it ever came into force — would almost automatically lead to the creation of a Scandinavian 'nuclear free zone' too. Yet it was equally significant that during the Federal election campaign, even the governing parties in Bonn left the details of the issue untouched. Public anxieties about nuclear dangers, made more acute by the Chernobyl incident, could well have re-opened an emotional debate about the implications for the country of its NATO membership. The Social Democrats likewise avoided bringing their 'agreement' with the East German governing party into the forefront of the election campaign, thus indirectly admitting that the whole idea was far from convincing for the majority of the population.

Norway's Social Democrats were able to withstand better than most the influence emanating from popular reaction to NATO's double-track decision. In fact, by the end of 1986, the deterrence posture of the Alliance in Norway looked rather more convincing that ever before. However, if a future United Kingdom Government were to abolish the British nuclear capability and ban US nuclear forces (cruise missiles and F-111 bombers) from Britain, NATO deterrence on the Northern Flank would immediately be affected. Militarily, alternatives would have to be found, but probably more important would be the psychological spill-over both on Peace movements and on the Social Democratic Parties, not only of Norway and Denmark, but also of the Federal Republic, the Netherlands and Belgium.

A Danish parliamentary and government decision to foreclose the nuclear option in the case of armed conflict would not only be embarrassing for NATO but would probably put the Norwegian Government under increased public pressure to do likewise. Given the geographical and strategic importance of both the northern member countries of NATO for the Alliance as a whole, one might nevertheless count on a degree of caution by Moscow. Of course, it would then depend very much on future administrations in Washington whether military and strategic planners in the Soviet Union perceived the Western Alliance as being so lacking in resolve as to let the Baltic Approaches or key areas of Norway fall into the hands of an attacker without resorting to nuclear warning strikes.

The years since 1979 have been particularly rich in lessons for NATO governments to learn, for political parties and for military planners as well. Any future administration in Washington must be aware that public opinion in the NATO countries, particularly in Northern and Central Europe, will, at all times, have to be convinced that the Alliance is pursuing efforts to bring about détente and disarmament (or at least arms control) with the same energy as it expends on trying to maintain credible deterrence. Each of the European NATO governments must be aware that by the interaction of public opinion and public moods, any marked change in national defence postures will have immediate effects in neighbouring member countries. Any major democratic opposition party must be aware that it shares the responsibility. The whole process of détente policy in the 70s proved that mutual concessions are unlikely to be reciprocated.

Military planners must also be aware that highly sensitive public opinion in Western Europe will not readily accept more defence programmes or new battle concepts foisted upon it without careful prior soundings involving experts of both governing and opposition parties. The democratic processes of NATO's sovereign states have to be fully respected, and smaller member nations in particular, like Denmark, Norway, the Benelux States and Greece, tend to appreciate it when they are given the attention due to them.

Rather unexpectedly, the Reykjavik summit meeting of President Reagan and General Secretary Mikhail Gorbachev launched a new public debate about the advantages or risks of trying to eliminate nuclear weapons. Few would contest vast reductions as a worthwhile aim in negotiations. But since Reykjavik, the question of conventional balance has come more sharply into focus than before. And it is this issue that carries more importance for NATO's Northern Flank even than it does for the Central Front.

Editor's Postscript

NO PLACE better demonstrates the dilemmas of European security than the Northern Flank. Here Norway and Denmark combine deterrence of any possibility of aggression or pressure by the Soviet Union with reassurance of Soviet fears in an attempt to give themselves the maximum degree of security. Right from the start, the Scandinavian members of NATO, scarred by the memory of foreign conquest but still not abandoning their neutralist traditions, clearly saw that a strong defence was only one aspect of a secure relationship with a threatening neighbour. A persistent recognition by the Norwegians and Danes of the legitimate security interests of the USSR has created unique conditions of co-existence in the North that are a model, perhaps, for what we ought to be aiming for right along the East–West divide. That all this can happen so close to the extraordinary concentration of military power that is the Kola Peninsula is especially significant. Of course, one should not over-state the degree of Soviet restraint. The Russians still find it hard to feel safe without dominating their neighbours in a disturbingly overbearing way. The repeated Soviet violations of Swedish coastal waters cannot but act as an example to both the Danes and Norwegians of the importance of maintaining a strong NATO guarantee of security.

As the last chapter has made clear, the maintenance of a proper compromise between defence and reassurance can be difficult politically, sometimes for the best of reasons, the tendency is to move too far towards the reassurance side of the equation. Reassurance, however, cannot work in an armed relationship if one side is unduly weak. Equally, unduly confrontationist attitudes can undermine the domestic defence consensus. The challenge in the North is how to maintain the working combination of strong and sufficient defence with a common regard for the other side's security while the rest of Europe catches up. Despite challenges like the growing importance of the Norwegian Sea in the global East–West naval confrontation, the auguries are positive. Mechanisms exist to tame and 'routinise' even the latter potentially explosive situation. Indeed, it may be a fortunate chance for world security that one of the Soviet Union's main vulnerable maritime pressure points is situated in a place where mutual threat is mitigated by a tradition of restraint. The image of the representatives of East and West shaking hands near Kirkenes, the one backed by the might of Soviet land power, the other by the newly reasserted strength of NATO maritime power projection is, in microcosm, the balance of power in Europe. That it is all so peaceful at the point of actual contact is both a vindication of the security policies of NATO's Northern European members over the last four decades and a source of hope and inspiration for all.

Index

Allied Command Europe Mobile Force Air (AMF(A)) 30, 33
Allied Command Europe Mobile Force Land (AMF(L)) 30-3
Allied Tactical Air Force 33
Anti-submarine warfare (ASW)
  in northern waters 9-12, 14, 80
  in the Baltic 80-1
Armed neutrality 92-3
Atlantic Command 3-6

Baltic Sea/region 11, 38-9, 71-81, 89, 98
  Baltic states 73
  Baltic strategy 71-81
BALTAP 38-9, 75-6, 79
Barents Sea 22, 29, 56
Belgium 35
Bornholm 78, 83-7
Bull-Hansen, General Fredrik 22

Canada 39, 81
  contributions to AMF(L) and AMF(A) 33
Carrington, Lord 96
Chernavin, Admiral 3

Damgaard, Knud 79
Denmark 4, 19, 71, 77, 89
  in Baltic 79-80
  defence policy 95-7, 101
  armed forces of 29-30
  and foreign bases/nuclear weapons 29, 89, 93-4, 96, 98
  see also Bornholm
Détente policy in the 70s 98
Dietl, General 66

Ellemann-Jensen, Uffe 96

Finland 54, 73, 89
  strength of forces 54

Garrod, Major-General Martin 41
German Democratic Republic (GDR) 73, 97
Germany, Federal Republic of (FRG)
  armed forces 80-1, 95-6
  contribution to AMF(L) 31, 33
  and defence of the North 96-7
  nuclear warheads on FRG territory 94-5
  SPD 94-7
GIUK gap (Greenland-Iceland-UK gap) 2, 4, 15, 48, 56
Gorbachev, Mikhail 3, 69, 98
Gorshkov, Admiral 3, 75

Hanseatic League 70
Heiberg-Jurgensen, Colonel 86-7
Helset, Major-General Gunnar 38, 40

Iceland 18-19
Italy and contribution to AMF(L) 32-3

Kekkonen, Urho 93
Kola Fortress 5, 7, 11-12, 22, 24, 47-70, 89
  population of 57, 66

Lehman, John 55
Luxembourg and contribution to AMF(L) 33

Memel-Mukran ferry 73-5

103

INDEX

NATO 2-4, 15, 24, 61, 76-81, 93-9
  Allied Command Europe Mobile Force Air (AMF(A)) 30, 33
  Allied Command Europe Mobile Force Land (AMF(L)) 30-3
  Allied Forces Northern Europe 28-9
  Allied Tactical Air Force 33
  Atlantic Command 3-6
    Tri-MNC concept 4-5
  convoy system 15-17
  exercises 3, 12-13, 16, 24-5, 27, 33-4, 36-7
  naval strategy 6
  security policies of N. European members 102
  Standing Naval Force Atlantic (STANAVFORLANT) 30, 34-6
  Striking Fleet 3-4, 6, 11-15
Netherlands, The 18
  contribution to AMF(A) 33
  UK/Netherlands Amphibious Force 39-41
Norway 2-3, 6, 9-13, 17, 21-30, 33-41, 43-57, 61-70, 75, 77, 89, 90-1, 101
  armed forces of 25-6
  and deterrence posture 97
  Finnmark, population of 57
  and foreign bases/nuclear weapons 29, 51, 89, 93-4, 98
  Norwegian Sea 19, 48-9, 101
  Norwegian-Soviet border 61-70
Nuclear-free zones 77, 94, 97

Palme, Olaf 93
Peace movements 98
Poland 29, 73
  1981-2 crisis 35
Polar region 56-7
Portugal 35

Reagan, Ronald 98
Rein, General Admiral 13
Reykjavik summit meeting 98-9
Rosnes, Major-General Arne 41

Schmidt, Helmut 94
Sjaastad, Anders 22, 49, 54

Soviet Union 2-4, 12, 22-3, 57-8
  fleets of 57-60
  Kola Fortress 5, 7, 11-12, 22, 24, 47-70, 89
  naval strategy of Northern Fleet 2-3
  Norwegian-Soviet border 61-70
  Spetsnaz (special forces) 53-4, 70
  submarines and bases 2-3, 7, 22-3, 47-8, 51, 54-6, 59, 77
  Summerex 1985 (exercise) 2-3, 24
Standing Naval Force Atlantic (STANAVFORLANT) 30, 34-6
Sweden 89
  and defence 90-3
  Soviet violations of neutral waters 77, 90, 101

Torhaug, Brigadier-General Inge 49, 62, 68-9
Treholt, Arne 90

United Kingdom 9-10, 14, 31, 33, 37-41, 43-6, 96-7
  commandos in Arctic training 43-6
  contributions to AMF(L) and AMF(A) 31, 33, 40
  and defence of the North 96-7
  Mobile Force (UKMF) 37-9
  and nuclear capability 97
  UK/Netherlands amphibious force 39-41
U.S.A.
  contributions to AMF(L) and AMF(A) 31, 33
  and defence of Iceland 18
  Marine Expeditionary Force (MEF) 37
  maritime strategy 6-9, 12
  submarines 57

Vaessen, Captain J. 4, 15
von Friedeburg, Admiral Georg 83
von Kamptz, Captain Gert 83-5

Warsaw Pact forces 29, 38, 77
  exercises of 2-3, 24, 48, 77
Watkins, Admiral James 7, 15, 57
Weinland, Robert 49
Whisky-on-the-rocks incident 90